Moving From Re[illegible]ater To Ready Now

Neil Raval David Smith

Moving From Ready Later To Ready Now

Cover design: Mike Thorpe at design-chapel.com

Published by Ready Now Publications

First published 2016

First Edition

a

ISBN: 978-0-9956733-0-4

Ordering Information:

Quantity sales: Special discounts are available on quantity purchases by corporations, associations, and others. For details, contact the publisher at the email address below.

editorRNP@ccmrconsulting.com

Printed in the United Kingdom

Contents

The reasons for reading this book

Today's world is highly competitive. Like it or not, you'll be expected to take control of your own career or run the risk of someone else being given the job you want, leaving you feeling overlooked.

The problem is, you are expected to take control but you are not given all the tools to do it. Things can feel worse when you start to realise that not taking control is regarded as a sign of weakness.

If you are ready to achieve the lifestyle you want by moving to your next job, or developing further in the one you already have, choose this book. It hands you the tools so you *can* take control.

By reading more you'll learn:

- How to decide what's next for you and how it fits with your life
- Who can help you, how to ask them, and how to build the relationships you need to succeed
- Practical ways to recognise your strengths, fill the gaps and manage your attitude
- How to become ready-now for your next role and prepare for recruitment discussions

If you're the manager of someone who is starting to take control of changing roles and want to help them in a time-efficient way, this book is for you too.

As a manager, you'll learn:

- How to make a career development conversation honest and useful
- Tactics to harness your normal, daily activities to support your staff's development
- How your feedback can make a difference
- Techniques for improving an individual's performance
- How your network can help your staff
- How these tools can help your career too

Introduction

How often do you see someone move ahead in his or her career and wonder why it isn't you? It can be frustrating and disappointing. You are just as dedicated, committed and hardworking yet they get chosen.

The key difference is that decision-makers see these colleagues as fully equipped and prepared, 'ready-now' for the next step.

You may well ask yourself the following questions:

- What have these people done to advance their career so successfully?
- How do decision-makers know these individuals are ready-now for their next challenge?
- How can I develop myself professionally to get the job and life I want?

This book has the answers. The simple tools and techniques enclosed will empower you to make extraordinary changes.

You'll change from operating on 'career auto-pilot' to seizing control of your working life and aspirations.

You'll change from missing opportunities to creating them for yourself.

You'll start to get noticed and earn respect for what you do now and, importantly, for what you could do next.

The valuable skills you'll learn will give you a competitive advantage not just in your career but also in life.

You will improve how you communicate, build relationships and influence others.

You will learn more about who you are, what you want in life and how to get the best support to achieve it.

You will become highly receptive and resilient to change and able to motivate yourself and those around you.

You will be happier doing your job, knowing you have a clear sense of where you want to be, and confident you are the kind of person others want to be with.

Moreover, you won't want to keep these skills and tools to yourself. You'll be eager to share them with those close to you so they will enjoy a happier, enriching and more successful career and life. That surely has to make you feel good?

There are valuable lessons within these pages for managers too.

A crucial role for any manager is to support staff in preparing for greater things. If you manage someone with their eye on a more senior role, you'll discover the tools to propel them on the road to promotion.

Many of the tools in this book have a wider application than simply helping people to move onwards and upwards.

They are just as effective for improving your team's performance and bolstering your organisation's relationships with key clients, partners and stakeholders.

We find these tools are not only simple and quick to use; they are highly infectious. Be assured, your leaders and peers will start to notice the impact you make by harnessing these fresh, new approaches and will be eager to capitalise on them too.

Wherever you sit in your organisation, implementing the lessons in this book will have a profound impact on you, your colleagues, your team and, ultimately, the success of your organisation.

The catalyst for this book

We enjoy meeting a challenge and this book was directly inspired by a challenge from a client and friend of ours. As a senior leader in a large corporation he found he was regularly sharing with others the skills and behaviours he'd learnt in our leadership and coaching workshops, to support their personal development. He noticed a trend: in the regularly changing organisation, most of his colleagues were missing the essential skills and behaviours which would help them move successfully from one job role to another. He explained:

"I need you guys to write down how to apply the skills you've taught me to the challenge of moving from one job to the next with some sense of direction. So many of the people I talk to feel stuck with the feedback 'you'll be ready-later for that job' and they feel puzzled about how to help themselves become ready-now. Write it all in a book so I can share the knowledge more quickly and give other people the chance to own and develop their careers as managers or employees."

To meet the challenge, we've drawn from our own experiences of being employees, managers and strategic leaders ourselves in large and small organisations. We've added inspirations from experts, authors, their books and their papers. We've married these with the experience and advice shared with us by the hundreds of wonderful people we've coached and taught in our coaching and leadership development workshops. All these are filtered to focus on what works and what doesn't work in the art of succeeding in a job and preparing for the next. We've pulled out our set of essential skills and behaviours which you'll find are straight-forward, reliable and surprisingly powerful.

Enjoy your read and let us know what changes *you* decide to make for yourself and what challenges you decide to meet.

To continue in the spirit of sharing what we learn, we'd like to hear your reflections and your own ideas for becoming ready-now, so we can include them in the next edition and help our readers become even more successful.

Now, look forward, take action and remember to enjoy the journey!

David M Smith, Neil V Raval.

DaveNeilRL2RN@ccmrconsulting.com

How to use this book

There are two main sections to the book.

Reading Part I, you will discover how to become ready-now for your next role. It is packed with straight forward tips and techniques which will provide solutions for you if the following sound familiar:

"It's time I thought seriously about my career"

"I need a change"

"My boss doesn't understand what I want"

"I've been overlooked"

"I feel ready for my next move and I need to make it happen"

"I've been told I need to 'own' my personal development"

"I need to get a grip on what I want to do next"

Part I will also help you recognise you are not alone in your mission to become ready-now and describes how to get the help you need.

If you are a manager yourself and want to learn more about how to help someone become ready-now, you can follow the references in Part I to the corresponding manager's skills in Part II. There, you'll find solutions to familiar questions such as:

"You're my manager and should be helping me more"

"You're their manager so you must help them find a new role in the re-organisation"

"What job do you think I should be doing next?"

"You're my boss and I trust you are looking after me and my career"

"What should I put in my development plan?"

Some of our readers find they like to read each chapter in sequence. Others get inspired by dipping excitedly into a random chapter and surprising themselves with what they discover. Do whatever's the most helpful for you!

Why ready later to ready now?

So, why have we used the phrase 'ready-later to ready-now'?

In many of our client organisations, individuals sit down for their performance review with their manager and are told they are not yet ready for their next role. Often there is a pause as they wait to be given a clue as to why, or what they need to change to become ready. Sometimes these clues are forthcoming, but often they aren't.

There are many myths associated with becoming ready for a role and we feel it's time we exploded a good many of them by describing the straight forward steps you can follow.

The terms ready-later and ready-now are often used within organisations as part of a career planning or succession planning approach. Individuals are evaluated by the organisation for their suitability in the next role in the career path they are following. Even in organisations which do not have such systematic approaches all managers develop some understanding of their staff and their capability to do whatever role comes next in their development. Ready-now usually means what it says, the individual is capable of moving into the next job now.

'Ready-later' can mean many things to many people. We describe someone as ready-later if they are able to develop to be ready for the next role within the next 6 to 12 months. This development relies partly on their capabilities and also on the availability of the support they need from those around them. If you hear yourself being described as ready-later you need to take immediate action to find, or develop, the steps which will develop you into a ready-now candidate. You will find the steps and inspiration you need in this book.

If, despite your best effort, you discover the development path is unlikely to exist, and there is no realistic opportunity for you to become ready-now for a specific role, it is time to review your options.

The brutal fact is many ready-later, ready-now decisions are not scientific or unbiased. Ready-later and ready-now are rarely the outcome of neutral evaluations with a battery of highly accurate tests. The allocation of the terms is more likely to be based on opinion and word of mouth. The good news is you can often work with influential opinion holders to modify their view and the opinions they share.

We encourage forward planning so remember that as soon as you become ready-now for one role you can start to become ready-later for your next role. Now, it's time to start thinking and planning for what you want to create next.

Part I

It's all about me

So, you are eager to take action and move yourself from being ready-later for a job role to being solidly ready-now. In the following chapters we have created 6 stages to help you focus your time on what matter most.

1. Knowing what role you want
2. Telling people what role you want
3. How to ask for help
4. Understanding your strengths and gaps
5. Preparing to fill, and filling, the essential gaps between what you have now and what you need
6. Taking action

1

Know the role you want

When you visit a shop to buy something, you'll increase your chances of success if you've got some idea of what you want to buy, or what you want to create. You may also feel inspired to buy a few items you hadn't planned for, and that inspiration feels good because it sits alongside knowing the basics of what you need.

No surprise then, when you are preparing to shop for your next role, you need to have some firm ideas of what you want, the timing, and how committed you are to getting it. This is a flavour of having a 'towards approach'.

So, take a towards approach: Decide what you want instead of what you don't want.

The opposite of a towards approach is the away-from approach which you will have experienced if you've ever heard someone say: "I don't want to stay on this salary", "I don't want to be under-appreciated", "I don't want to be all-work-and-no-play", "I don't want to stay in this job for ever", "I don't want to live here" or "I don't want my boss to get in the way of my progress". An away-from example like "I don't want to live here" sounds meaningful at first, and can encourage some action and change. However, it lacks a sense of direction and, as we coach our clients, it encourages us to ask:

"How will you know if the change will be what you want or need?"

Any change can bring disadvantages as well as advantages so having a good understanding of what you *do* want can help you balance the result in favour of the advantages. In this example, better results will come from saying:

"I don't want to live here. I want to live in the city, 10 minutes walk from the station, in a two-bed flat, with rent which leaves me enough to socialise twice a week and pay my bills."

Similarly, if you have an expectation of "I don't want my manager to get in the way of my progress" you have set an away-from target and can take action to achieve this. But how much more successful could you be if you apply towards-thinking and decide "I want my manager to *help* me make the progress I need"?

So, decide and tell those around you the positive side: what you do want.

More than just a title

99 percent of job hunters only use a job title when they are talking about the new role they want. What's wrong with that?

When we hear a job title, we focus on where that job title may exist and where vacancies with that title occur.

That focus can be helpful to some degree, but it also restricts our job search results because there will be other jobs requiring very similar skills but with a different title.

Tip: Describe what's in the role you want. By telling people what elements the job role actually consists of, you may trigger new ideas which are not constrained by official job titles.

We learned the benefits of this when a client, John, described to his manager what was inside the role he was looking for. His manager replied:

"Ok John, you want the role to include organising things, some technical specialism and working with many people in teams. Well, we haven't got any of the project manager vacancies you talked about, but we do have an account manager role which has what you are looking for, how does that sound?"

You can read more about this technique in the section Have a towards approach on page 77.

Know the role you want: fitting work and life together

If you ask someone what is important to them about their job, you will get an answer connected to the priority they place on their own personal values. Someone in their first job may immediately answer "money is the most important thing", whereas a new parent may say "flexibility, so I can earn while also being home when the children need me." Equally, someone approaching retirement may answer "giving something back, mentoring and supporting people who need a little help."

Before you decide what your next role will be, take some time, now, to check how your role must fit in with other important parts of your life. The circle in the picture describes key aspects of life.

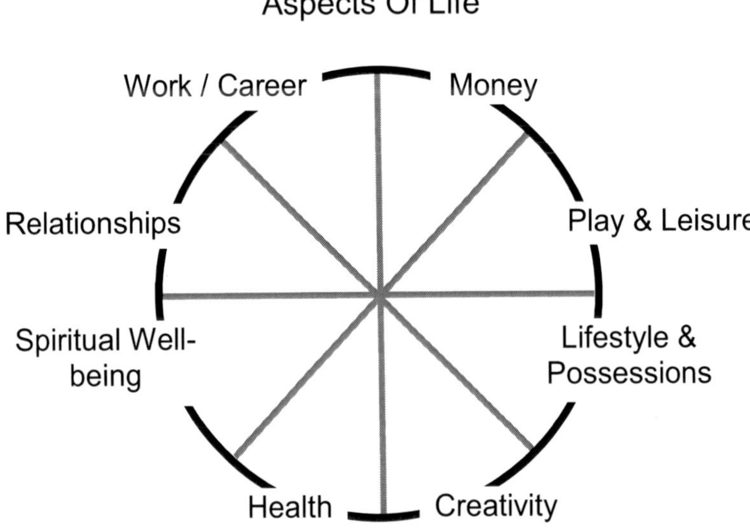

Look at each segment and make a note of your current situation and any change you'd like to make for improvement. For example:

Current situation: I'm in good health but not doing anything to maintain it.

A change I'd like to make: I will exercise twice a week.

There's a template to capture your notes in the appendix on page 288.

Ask yourself: Which parts of my life are most important to me now? There's no right and wrong, it's simply your choice and you can change it over time. Use your most important life segments to influence how you describe your next role, for instance: "My next role will focus on earning a high income, but it must allow me two or more evenings a week free for exercise."

"I don't think of work as work and play as play. It's all living."
Richard Branson

Know the role you want: Acknowledge your core values

We each have our own set of fundamental values which guide and affect the way in which we live our lives and respond to other individuals and organisations. Our core values are important to us and help describe what we believe in. We develop these values from a combination of our upbringing and life experiences. It is important to consider how these values could or should affect your choices as you look for a change of role. Examples of core life values include:

- An association with a religious belief
- Looking after the environment locally and beyond
- Placing family first in our priorities
- Honesty is always the best policy
- A healthy life has work-life balance

To help you explore your own values and describe them in words, we recommend you use the short exercise in the appendix Core Values Quiz on page 289. If you're already clear about your values, use the quiz to check whether the priority of your values have shifted over time.

As individuals, we developed our personal core values to guide us. Similarly, many leaders have developed a set of core values to guide their organisation. Their core values are designed to build respect and a positive reputation with employees, investors, customers and suppliers. As you plan to change role, compare your values with those of each organisation which interests you, and decide whether the organisation's core values encourage you towards them, or have the opposite effect.

Here are the corporate values of several organisations you may know:

Barclays bank describes its core values as Respect, Integrity, Service, Excellence and Stewardship.

Environmental sustainability is a core value of Patagonia and Ben & Jerry's and one of Starbucks' six core values is 'Contribute positively to our communities and our environment'.

At the Build-A-Bear Workshop company 'Di-bear-sity' was the most recent value to be added. It was selected and named via a 2012 company-wide contest.

Toyota has four core values: customer first, respect for people, international focus and continuous improvement and innovation.

Google has 10 core value statements which can be summarised as making a great search engine and building a great company without doing evil.

The British Royal Air Force core values are Respect, Integrity, Service and Excellence.

For large institutions, it is quite easy to find these statements with a quick internet search. It may take more research to discover the core values for a smaller organisation or a specific department, and how they are demonstrated at a local level. You can find this out by talking to those already employed by the organisation, or those who interact with it.

Make the core values comparison

If your core values match those of the organisation you wish to join, it is likely you will find a common purpose, and find your role more fulfilling and satisfying. Equally if there is a strong mismatch this can lead to stress and frustration for you and the employer.

Remember to find out how the organisation will want you to deliver the new role, so you understand whether that fits well for you too.

A mismatch will occur, for example, when someone who believes that family time is critically important accepts a role requiring them to travel from country to country for eight months a year based on plans which regularly change at short notice. An immediate personal conflict is created immediately. Similarly, if someone with strong environmental beliefs joins a company known as a polluter there will be conflict and frustration.

Of course, there can be situations when a mismatch is appropriate as long as it is a conscious choice. For example:

- **When introducing change to an organisation**. A new CEO, with strong environmental beliefs, joins an organisation known for its pollution, and uses his influence to remove pollutants and build a 'clean' reputation for the company.

- **When joining an organisation as a 'stepping stone'**: A teacher with a strong drive to work in a government-funded school takes a two-year contract in a privately funded school to build experience and a strong CV to support them moving to a government-funded school later.

As you decide the role you want, remember, it's not just about the job you want to do, it's about who you want to be.

"Values are not like laws – you cannot break them.
You can only break yourself against them."
Mark Wright

Know the role you want: How a coach and a mentor can help

We are not alone in our work and life but it's surprising how many of us act as though we have to solve everything ourselves. Often there are people who could help us, if only we asked them. So, we encourage you to ask!

There are no guarantees in life but asking does increase your chances of getting what you need. In a job context, talking to someone can help you recognise your strengths and gaps, and help you understand the role you really want so you can decide what steps you need to take to get it.

There are two styles of conversation which will help you with this: a mentoring conversation and a coaching conversation. Each offers something different.

During a mentoring conversation, the mentor expects you to ask them for advice because they have been chosen for possessing the skills, knowledge, experience or relationships you need.

During a coaching conversation, you are asking the coach to encourage your own thinking, inspire you to have new ideas, unlock your mental blocks, and to help you arrive at your own plan, feeling motivated and in control.

Both styles are valuable and have their own distinct advantages when used at the right time.

Use the following summaries to help you decide, in different circumstances, whether coaching or mentoring is what you need. Use them to find exactly the right person to speak to.

The coaching style

- Asks questions
- Focuses on goals or outcomes
- Focuses on the coachee
- Coach chosen independent of skills and knowledge
- Coachee owns the outcomes

The mentoring style

- Tells, gives opinions, provides answers
- Focuses on skills or experience
- Focus is often on the mentor
- Mentor chosen because of their skills and knowledge
- Mentor follows up on delivery

Have a mentoring conversation when …

- You need a quick start
- You need to boost your knowledge about a subject
- You want to understand what expectations you need to meet
- Quoting an influential expert will influence others

Have a coaching conversation when …

- You need to clarify your thinking and increase your confidence in what you know
- You want to open up different solutions or novel thinking
- You want to explore options
- You're not exactly sure how to describe your opportunity or problem

The differences between coaching and mentoring can be compared to using use a map compared to a satnav. With a map you can take the overview, explore and decide where you want to go, and you make choices about how you get there. With a satnav, you are presented with the route and you are given directions to get you from A to B; you have little control over the route chosen and you are following the instructions you're given.

Both types of conversation can help you in your decision-making. Just be clear that the final decision is yours and you need to feel a level of well-grounded confidence in your choice.

Check the role you want exists or could exist

When you know what role you'd like to do, but there isn't a vacancy being formally advertised, check to make sure the role you want exists (though it may be occupied), or will become available, within the organisation in a reasonable period of time. Ask questions to find out if this is the case. We know of colleagues who became increasingly frustrated because the role they desperately wanted was being occupied by someone who was planning to stay in the job for the foreseeable future. They eventually recognised their options were to achieve a different role, move to a different department, or change company altogether.

While it is unreasonable to expect an organisation to change its strategy and create an unnecessary role simply to suit your career aspirations, it is often very possible to negotiate a role which works for both you and for the organisation.

In organisations of all sizes there is an investment necessary to bring in new employees, and to support them in reaching a good level of productivity.

If you choose to leave, you take that investment with you. Instead of losing the investment your employer may decide to work with you to negotiate a change of role. That way, you will be more motivated at work and the company continues to benefit from their investment.

Chapter review

Now you have the facts, you are equipped to explain clearly to people what role you want. The next stage is to tell them.

Before you do, pause and ask yourself the following questions, based on what you have read in chapter 1. Doing this helps you make your ideas and decisions clearer and strengthens your learning.

Knowing what role you want

- How does your next role need to fit alongside other priorities in your life?
- What are your core values?
- How do your core values fit with the role you want?
- How do your core values fit with the organisation(s) you are considering?
- How could a mentor help you?
- How could a coach help you?

2

Tell people what role you want

They are not mind-readers!

Do you remember ever opening your birthday presents and, despite receiving some lovely gifts, you were left feeling a little dissatisfied? Later you realise you had very clear ideas about the presents you wanted to receive, but you didn't tell anyone. You wanted them to work it out for themselves.

When we step back and take a look at our lives in the whole, this is a pattern which repeats for a lot of us on a regular basis. We carry an expectation that those around us are mind-readers. We expect them to know what we want from them. This even applies in the world of work. You may overhear the complaint "He should have known I'd be interested in that job" or "She didn't even let me know the applications for the job were closing tomorrow. I wanted to be considered for it". When we are coaching someone and hear a similar kind of statement, we constructively challenge them with a question such as "When did you tell them you were interested in this type of role?" or "When did you ask them to consider you for their vacancy?" A period of silence often follows as they reflect on their inaction.

Many of us can be reticent in clearly telling people what we actually want. Maybe we believe it is rude or presumptuous. Maybe we don't think the other person has the power to give us what we want and we don't want to embarrass them. Perhaps we're just shy or judge the people who do it as pushy. Whatever the reason, we seem to hold back from sharing what we want clearly with others.

From a manager's perspective, it's much easier to help someone who is clear about what they want.

The manager then has ideas to build on. They can give constructive feedback. They can feel energised by giving their time and resources to someone who seems to know what they want and has a determination to achieve it.

The alternative (giving your manager some vague hints and not asking directly) means they will make assumptions about what you want. They may even add what they think you *should* want to do. If you have some well-developed ideas in your head, you may be able to battle against their assumptions and direct them towards your own thinking. But there's a risk you won't succeed, or they interpret your challenges as unhelpful and lose their motivation to help you. With their assumptions and your own vagueness in play, it's clear this is not an effective strategy for developing your career.

If a manager has to choose between investing time in someone who has explained exactly what they want, and investing in someone who expects them to guess, who are they more likely to choose? Most of us would choose the simpler option, especially in today's busy world.

By telling someone what you want you make their lives easier. You increase the chances of getting what you want, or finding out what you need to do to get it.

So now you know you need to ask, here's how can you ask in a positive way, to maximise your chance of getting what you want.

Ask for what you *do* want

Ask for what you *do* want, seems like a very obvious statement, yet many don't do it. They invest more time talking about what's wrong, what they'd like to stop and what they don't want.

It's always more powerful to describe what you do want rather than what you don't want. If you were in a café asking for a hot drink you could say "I don't want a coffee or a hot chocolate or anything with milk in it please." You have given some information but the server will still be guessing which of the available alternatives you want.

Be precise in what you are asking for

It's important to be crystal clear about what you are asking for, otherwise you can end up describing what you want in such a vague way that you still leave the other person guessing. This makes it very hard for them to offer their help.

For example, imagine someone, let's call him Steffan, is starting a career discussion with his manager. It may go like this:

Steffan: "I'd like a bit of help with my next career step please."

Manager: "Of course, what would you like your next step to be?"

Steffan: "Well I've been thinking about it. I want something exciting, and not too boring. You know what I mean. It's got to stretch me without stressing me too much. I'd like to work on my own, with customers perhaps, but working in a team would be good too. Everybody says there are good opportunities around and I want one of the new roles. I'm always up for a challenge, as you know, so I want to work with the best. I was talking to one of my friends and he said that was very important for my long term career progression. So I'd like you to help me achieve this. And I'd like to get there as soon as possible."

Manager: "Huh ?"

You can easily see Steffan hasn't asked his manager for anything specific. Instead he's been incredibly vague and imprecise which leaves his manager with the challenge of working out what the question really is before he can offer his help.

The risk to Steffan is his manager will feel the challenge of working out the question is too much like hard work, alongside all the other calls on his time. Another risk of being vague like this, to a time-poor manager, is they leap to a conclusion for themselves and launch into helping in a way which may not be helpful at all.

Steffan could benefit significantly more from his manager's limited time if he made his request for help more precise.

Preparing, before asking for help is a simple but valuable step you can take. Write down what you are asking for so you can check for vague words, notice where they occur and replace them with more precise language.

You'll learn how to remove vagueness, and strengthen your precision on page 105.

If we replay Steffan's request to his manager with more precision, it may go like this:

Steffan: "I'd like a bit of help with my next career step please."

Manager: "Of course, what would you like your next step to be?"

Steffan: "Well, I've been thinking about where I want to go next in my career and you know I'm eager to earn my next role, so I want to move into one at any point from June onwards.
I want something which includes international working and contact with one of our three major blue chip clients because I find that idea exciting and the cultural differences interest me. Talking to Mike and Andy in the account management team, their roles sound stretching and a manageable challenge for me."

Steffan: "The account management section is seen as one of the best in the company and my mentor says working in a department with that kind of profile will help my long term career.
I'd like your opinion of how well I could fit into this kind of role and what other roles, which I might not be aware of, will have similar characteristics."

In this revised version Steffan has described the role he wants with sufficient precision that his manager's understanding is likely to be very close to his own, giving them both a strong starting point.

At the end of this version Steffan has also been much more specific about how exactly he'd like his manager to help him, so Steffan's more likely to get the help he really needs.

As you collect your thoughts about precisely what you want, remember to add some ideas about what type of help you'd like someone to give you. The clearer we can be about the type of help we need, the more likely we are to have a useful conversation.

"Ask for what you want
and be prepared to get it!"
Maya Angelou

3

How to ask for different types of help

There are many different types of help a person can offer you, so it's important to first decide what help you need. It could be:

- Advice
- Feedback
- An introduction
- Time for self development
- Information about a job's characteristics
- Contact information
- Application form help
- Help to raise your visibility
- Career review
- Early warning of new vacancies

Add to this list any extra types of help which are relevant to you and decide which may apply to the people you will ask.

This small preparation step can be very valuable if the person you are asking doesn't immediately feel they can help. If that's the case, you can ask them for a different type of help, one which they can provide more easily.
For example:

"Raj, I'd like some advice from you about how to become a project manager"

"Sorry, I know lots about being a project analyst but it's not the same thing"

"Ok. Thanks. Who could you introduce me to, so I can find out more?"

Asking clearly for what you want, or describing what you are looking for, gives the other person some information to build on. They may even offer further help as well.

Explain your reason for asking

If you ask for a type of help and add the reason you are asking, the reason may give the other person the opportunity to suggest alternative ways in which they could help, or alternative sources of help. For example, you could ask:

"Sue, I'd like you to introduce me to Andy next time he's in the office."

Let's assume Sue agrees to make introduction and that's where it ends. If she had time, she might ask about the reason for the introduction. At that point Sue's having to invest her time to work out what you want. It is much easier for her if, instead, you include some context or reason:

"Sue, I'm exploring the idea of moving to an account manager role. I'd like you to introduce me to Andy next time he's in the office so he knows me when I ask for a chat about the role."

Sue is now aware of the reason for the introduction and so may also introduce you to two or three other people who can help.

Feel confident in asking for help. You'll be surprised at how many positive responses you receive.

A study in 2008 by Stanford Graduate School of Business highlights how we underestimate the likelihood of receiving help. Their research found participants predicted they would have to ask 50% more people for help than the actual number needed. The research leader, Frank Flynn, associate professor of organisational behaviour at Stanford GSB, explains that "People's underestimation of others' willingness to comply is driven by their failure to diagnose [the] feelings of social obligation on the part of others." In general, people like to help, and want to be seen as helpful.

Another Stanford GSB study discovered there's a big difference between how we feel we should ask for help and how we like to receive a request for help when we have something to offer. Those asking for help felt an indirect approach, using a certain look or a subtle hint, would be more successful than asking a direct question. Those who were being asked for the help said they were much more likely to agree when asked for help clearly and directly and even more so if asked face to face.

4

Deciding who to ask for help

When you think about who can help you in your career development be sure to think broadly. A common approach is to only ask a line manager. That may be a good place to start for you. Keep going though and find other people-of-influence, or 'stakeholders', who are available to you.

A stakeholder can be described as 'a person or group with an investment, share, or interest in something'.

Project managers often talk about carefully working with stakeholders who can help them complete their project successfully. The project manager needs each stakeholder to show commitment to the project goals, and provide their expertise or influence. Your career is a project of yours, and you too can increase your success by identifying and managing stakeholders who can help. Your stakeholders can assist you to persuade the 'gatekeepers' of a role that you are the right person to choose.

Identify who can influence your success

In many organisations, individuals will not be considered for an internal job vacancy, or further personal development, unless one or more influential people, or gatekeepers, have given their approval, either formally or informally.

Who are the gatekeepers controlling or influencing the role you are aiming for?

This is a key list for you to create and the task of identifying them may be surprisingly straightforward once you begin to search.

Common examples of where to find these influencers are:

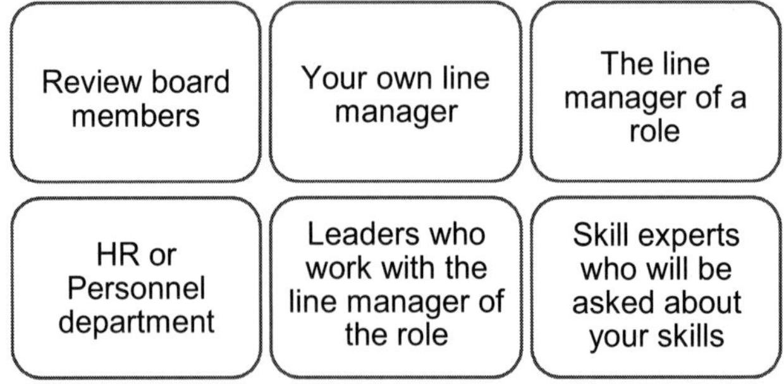

When you know who these gatekeepers are, it is time for you to influence them to make decisions in favour of you.

There are two routes to influencing them: either directly or indirectly.

To influence them directly you will need to contact them, explain what you want, and persuade them you are the right person for the role.

To influence them indirectly you will need to engage the help of someone else, a stakeholder who, in turn, will help influence the decisions to be made in favour of you.

To identify stakeholders who could help you, read the questions below and note the names of everyone you know who fits in each category.

- Who is enthusiastic to get the specific job vacancy filled?
- Who has an interest in helping you make progress in your career (either for altruistic purposes or because they will somehow benefit from the change)?
- Who has an interest in passing on their knowledge to you
- Who has an interest in making useful connections between individuals (eg. between you and someone who has a vacancy, or skills or influence which would be helpful to you)?
- Who is willing to recommend you to others because they have confidence in you and in what you do?

Once you have constructed your stakeholder list ask yourself how these people can help you and what help you need from them.

It may be by providing feedback on your strengths and areas for development, or assistance with introductions. It may be sharing their knowledge of the organisation or their understanding of a role. In the case of family and friends think about what support can they give you and who they know. We often find asking family and friends for help and support is overlooked.

Finally, decide how you will ask for the help you need.

- What direct request are you going to make and when will you make it?
- When might be the most appropriate time to talk to each stakeholder? During social events? After a meeting? Follow their preference.

To help you structure your approach with each stakeholder we've created the following template, with examples which will prompt your planning.

Stakeholder Management Plan

Stakeholder Name	Ash Drew
What is their position in relation to what I want to achieve?	Colleague of a gatekeeper
How can they help me? What help do I need from them?	They have good relationship with Shen, a gatekeeper. They can introduce me to Shen
What am I going to ask them for?	To ask Shen to meet me for 30 minutes to help me understand the department priorities
What type of approach do they prefer? (formal or informal, face to face or email)	Informal conversation in office
When am I going to ask them?	Wednesday

Building and maintaining stakeholder and gatekeeper relationships

Having identified your current stakeholders, you may notice a gap. For example, one of our clients discovered she did not have any stakeholders who could help her influence a key gatekeeper in a department where she wanted to work. She decided to build a working relationship with a stakeholder who was in the same leadership team as the gatekeeper.

With help from her new stakeholder she was introduced to the gatekeeper, meeting him for a cup of coffee and a discussion about how the department was organised and the key roles. A coffee conversation is often a good way of reducing the perceived formality of the discussion and in this case the gatekeeper was happy to have the conversation without there being any vacancy advertised.

A proactive discussion, before any vacancy is advertised, is often preferable because it gives you the opportunity to talk to the gatekeeper when they aren't distracted by responding to vacancy applicants. Talking to them also demonstrates you are actively interested in managing your own career, which is a positive impression to develop.

Before you meet a gatekeeper, remember to prepare for your discussion. It is not unknown for these informal chats to become at least the first stage of an interview process, without any warning. You can read more about this in the chapter Gap: I need to prepare for talking to recruiting managers on page 143.

Do some research to understand the basic facts about the person you are going to talk to, and facts about the organisation and skillset they manage.

Use these questions to help you prepare for the discussion:

Search for these answers by talking to people you know and by searching online. If you can't find out an answer in advance you can ask the question when you meet.

To help you decide the content of the conversation itself, use these prompts:

- What do you need from the person as a result of your conversation?
- What skills, knowledge, and experience do you bring?
- What makes you uniquely you and well suited for the kind of role you are looking for?
- What do you want to develop, in yourself, by taking on your next role?
- What do you want to know about a role or potential role?

Finally, think forward to the end of the conversation. Decide what, at that point, you want them to know, feel and do as a result of meeting you. If you want to challenge yourself more, decide what you want them to tell other people about you, and about your discussion.

Prepare a short summary of key points which you can re-play at the end of the conversation to make sure the person is clear about what you want. Before you finish, share some positive reflections about what you have learned from the meeting.

You can apply a similar approach to prepare for a discussion with a stakeholder, to develop and maintain the relationship, and to make the most of each conversation.

Remember that relationships are very seldom built with one contact. You need to invest time in maintaining the relationship and potentially developing it further by communicating regularly.

Become more visible to Gatekeepers

Before some Gatekeepers will consider you for a role they will want you to have been 'visible' to them so they have some personal experience of who you are and how you do what you do. That experience is an important convincer for them. If they do not know who you are, you will be at a major disadvantage. If you receive feedback that suggests you need to 'increase your visibility' or 'raise your profile' it is because someone in the decision-making chain needs to feel they know more about you before they make a decision.

Neil learned about this the hard way in his early career. He focused his efforts on his work and, after a succession of positive performance review discussions, his manager lobbied more senior decision makers to agree a promotion for him. The application was refused with the reason that Neil's 'profile wasn't high enough.'

By asking a few questions, his manager discovered that one of the influential decision-makers had never worked with Neil. The decision-maker was only prepared to support progression for staff he knew personally. Neil's manager made sure that Neil's next assignment would put him in direct contact with this decision-maker and, sure enough, the next time the application for promotion was made, Neil received the promotion without challenge.

Who do *you* need to be more visible to, and how will you accomplish that visibility?

Options may include delivering a successful piece of work for them, or making a presentation while they are in the audience. It could be ensuring they have seen reports with your name on, or have met you as a member of a project team. Some decision-makers need to get to know you as a person as well as an employee to raise their confidence. Different individuals have different preferences, so it is important to find out what convincers your stakeholders need.

Successful routes to discovering their convincer preferences include:

- Observing who has been successful in influencing them and what steps they used
- Asking staff who have worked with the individual recently
- Asking your manager
- Directly asking the individual what you need to demonstrate so that they will consider you for a role or promotion

Read more about increasing your visibility on page 135.

Giving gifts as well as asking

The asking for help chapters have been solidly focused on just that: You asking for help and expecting to get the help you ask for. All very one directional.

A simple way of redressing this balance, and building a greater chance of receiving the help you ask for, is 'giving gifts'. As humans, we are much more likely to give things to someone when the person requesting has done something for us, or is someone we regard as being generous towards others.

What could you be doing to be seen as a generous person?

Your generosity can be demonstrated by simply taking discretionary actions which help others around you. For example, taking the time to help a colleague research a subject they are about to write a report on; using your contacts to help someone else resolve a problem they are having; making introductions for someone; or even being the person who brings cakes in for the office on a Friday afternoon.

A relative of Dave's used this tactic highly effectively when she was recruited into a temporary job within a company where she wanted to work permanently.

She went out of her way to help each of her colleagues and baked delicious cakes for the office every week. The team came to see her as a core member of the office and, when a permanent vacancy was advertised, she immediately had the support of her other team members and was given the promotion.

Who do you see giving gifts of their time and skills? What could you be giving more of, to raise your visibility?

Of course, your time is a precious commodity so be careful about controlling how much time you invest in gift giving. Give when you can, without interfering with what is expected of you. And help yourself by making sure some of your gift giving is carefully targeted.

Target some of your giving towards individuals you wish to influence directly or where your help will be visible to the person you wish to influence. You can also target your help so those you wish to influence hear about it through those they talk to.

Chapter review

So far, you have strengthened your knowledge about the role you want and have the tools for telling others about what you want and for asking for their help.

Reflect on what you have discovered by asking yourself the following questions, based on what you have read in chapters 2, 3 and 4. This will, again, help you make your ideas and decisions clearer and strengthen your learning.

Telling people what role you want and asking for help

- What are the key messages for your manager?
- Who else do you need to tell?
- What help do you want?
- What do you want to ask for?
- What do you want to ask for first?
- Who else will you ask for something?
- Who are the gatekeepers you need to influence?
- Who do you need to be more visible to?
- How will you increase your visibility?
- What gifts do you already give?
- What further gifts can you give to others?

5

Understanding your strengths and gaps

You will already have valuable skills, behaviours and relationships, so be honest with yourself about the strengths you have, and the gaps you need to fill, to get the role you want.

Take some time to understand what is needed for the role and compare what you find with what you have today.

How do you go about doing this? Use the following steps:

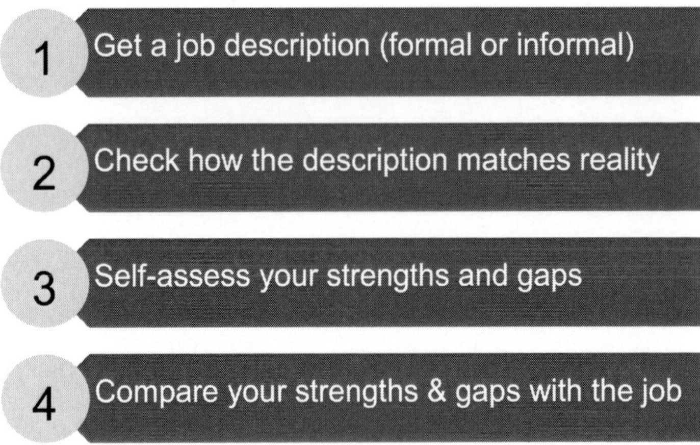

1
Get a job description (formal or informal)
2
Check how the description matches reality
3
Self-assess your strengths and gaps
4
Compare your strengths & gaps with the job

We'll dip into each of these to highlight how to approach each step.

Get a job description (formal or informal)

You may find there is a formal job description for the role which interests you. If the job isn't currently being advertised, then you can search past advertisements, talk to the HR function in your organisation, or ask someone who currently holds the role or manages the role holder.

Check how the description matches reality

When you read the documented requirements of a job you'll often find a long list of essential and desirable skills. It is amazing how often these lists seem to demand someone with superhuman qualities to fulfil them! If you, like most people, are not equipped with x-ray vision and the ability to leap over tall buildings, then it's worth taking a reality check. You can read more about how to do this on page 41.

Self-assess your strengths and gaps

Prepare yourself for this step by listening to what you tell yourself, (i.e. your self-talk) when you think about your strengths and the gaps. You need to strike a balance between telling yourself exaggerated positive things "I'm very skilled at eating biscuits" and telling yourself the brutal facts "I had twenty biscuits today, again, which is not good for me." Avoid the risk of overemphasising your limitations too; change "I will never be able to control the number of biscuits I eat" to "I haven't yet found a successful way to control the number of biscuits I eat."

You will find more tips about harnessing the power of your self-talk on page 119.

To create your self-assessment, make a note of your strengths and gaps. Later you can compare these with the job descriptions which interest you, to determine which skills you need to maintain and which to develop further.

A quick search online will help you find lots of templates to help you structure your self-assessment notes. Alternatively, you can use and adapt the template in the appendix on page 291.

Compare your strengths and gaps with the job

You are now in a position to be armed with an understanding of what's needed in the role you want, plus your self-assessment of your strengths and gaps, supported by the feedback you have collected. You can now compare what you personally bring to a job with the entry-level expectations of the job you want.

As you make your comparison, review your skills analysis and ask yourself how the categories below assist you in recognising more strengths. We've added a few examples in italics.

My knowledge	*Up to date knowledge of latest DNA sequencing techniques*
My experience	*Managing projects with budgets totalling up to $50,000*
My behaviours	*Patient. Curious. Quick decision-making, building relationships*
My personal Values	*Honesty. Fairness.*

Make a note of which strengths match well with the job you are aiming for and which gaps you will need to pay attention to. Use the following sections in this chapter as a reminder to work out *which* skills you really need and what *level* of the skills are necessary for the early stages of a role.

Which skills do I really need?

Have you noticed some job descriptions seem to be describing a superwoman or superman? The list of required skills and experience is so extensive, you start to wonder if anyone really has all these abilities!

Here's the reason, explained by Kurt, a manager in a large corporation:

"When I create a job description I write down all the skills and experience the job needs now, then I write down extra skills which will help grow the job.

The growth skills may be chosen because I know how the job will develop, or maybe because there is a lot of uncertainty about how the job will change over time.

When I recruit someone into the company, I'm not expecting them to stay in the same job for ever, even if it does develop. So, I will add extra behaviour skills into the job description.

Those skills will give the successful candidate the opportunity to develop their role beyond the job I'm recruiting for."

You can understand then, how job descriptions can become bloated with skills, knowledge and experience.

Your task is to find out which are the minimum requirements for the role. The rest is often negotiable. Some recruiters will make this task easier for you by dividing the job description requirements into a list of 'minimum requirements' and a list of 'highly desired requirements.'

Jane described to us how she was offered a new role after deciding to apply, even though she didn't have all the required skills:

> "I looked at the job description and felt I'd got some of the minimum requirements, but three requirements were for experience of technical tools I didn't know.
>
> In the highly desirable requirements I did meet, one was experience in the type of manufacturing I've worked in a lot, and another was being able to create successful relationships between multiple teams. I've done that a lot too.
>
> I asked the recruiters to find me someone to speak to who knew the job and how it needed to be done. I learned what was really needed was someone who could work across teams, building connections and relationships, because poor relationships between teams was getting in the way of success.
>
> I decided to apply and talked a lot about my work connecting teams. After the interview, I was told they decided the hardest thing to find was someone with my experience of manufacturing plus an ability to craft good relationships. They asked if I'd be prepared to take some training to give me the knowledge of the technical tools, if they offered me the job. I said yes! The experienced helped me recognise the importance of some of my strengths which I hadn't even realised were strengths. It also reminded me that it's always worth hearing what is really important in a job before applying."

What level of the key skills are needed for a role?

Now you're aware that some of the skills, knowledge and experience in a role description may be negotiable. You can build on your strengths and add further, required, skills 'on the job.' Be aware too, the *level* or strength of skills, knowledge and experience needed for a role can vary for each role.
These levels can be described as:

Basic Awareness : Aware of the competencies (skills, knowledge and experience) needed for a role, perhaps from talking about it or reading about it. The competencies haven't yet been demonstrated.

Basic Competency : Basic understanding of the competencies and able to use the relevant terminology. Able to handle routine tasks. May need guidance from someone who knows the role.

Proficient : Sufficiently strong in the necessary competencies to be consistently demonstrating success in the role. Able to handle routine and non-routine activities with minimal guidance. Able to assist others in their application of the relevant competencies.

Advanced: Skills, knowledge and experience are highly developed, and there's an ability to teach others and apply the competencies more holistically – knowing how the role fits with other roles and situations.

Expert: An authority, recognised by others as a go-to source. Able to creatively develop new applications of the competency, and can develop a vision for how a competency will develop in the future.

In an entry-level role, you may be expected to have an *awareness* of some requirements and a *basic competency* in others. In a role as an expert, expectations may be higher. However, remember:

- Test out your assumptions about the levels of skills, knowledge and experience required in a role. Ask questions! One recruiting manager's expectations of '*proficient'* may be very different from another.

- Be honest in describing the level of skills you possess.

- There is no excuse for you contacting someone about a role and admitting you have 'no' experience. If there's a job requirement you know nothing about, take the simple step of searching online and reading about the subject to move your competency from 'none' to 'basic awareness'.

Be prepared to further develop your level of competency when you start your new role. The expectation of how you use your skills, and how you behave, will generally rise as you become more established.

A former manager taught Dave about this change in competency level. His manager accepted that Dave's entry-level skills in a new job would be adequate for a time, and provided clues about what could change for the better.

Dave explains it like this:

"After being in several monthly leadership team meetings, I asked my manager if I was speaking-out enough. He replied 'Oh yes. You're saying plenty and you'll improve over time.' When I asked how I could improve, his simple answer was 'Give it some time, and listen more to what the others are saying.'

When I asked again, three months later, his tone was upbeat. 'Yes, good job. You've stopped just telling us what you know. You're curious what the others say, and that interest makes them want to work with you. That's how this team is so successful: because of how we work together.'"

When you plan to start a new role, find out which level of the skills and behaviours are important to demonstrate from the start. Concentrate on these as a priority, rather than attempting to do everything perfectly at once. As Dave did, ask for feedback to give you clues about how you can improve, and decide what action you will take on what you hear.

Chapter review

Now you know the role you want, and you have the tools to tell others what you want and to ask for their help. You also understand your strengths and gaps.

This is an important milestone, so reflect on what you have discovered by asking yourself the following questions, based on what you've read in this chapter. This will, again, help you make your ideas and decisions clearer and strengthen your learning.

Understanding your strengths and gaps

- What do you now understand about the job you want?
- What are your key strengths and gaps?
- Which skills, knowledge and experience are *most* essential to have for the role you want?
- To begin the role, what is the minimal level you will need to have of each?
- How do these align with your current key strengths and gaps?

6

Collecting and learning from feedback

Use feedback to stay honest about your strengths and gaps

Once you have created your own skills self-assessment, you will want to know how closely your opinion of your strengths and gaps matches the opinion of others who know you. This step brings an honesty to your assessment, making it more valuable to you as an accurate starting point for planning your move to your next role.

A good way of learning more about your strengths and gaps is by asking for feedback.

There may have been times in the past when you only wanted to hear people say good things about what you do. However, if we are genuinely interested in making progress in our careers, we need to recognise that feedback can highlight strengths we've been unaware of, and important gaps, which can then be addressed to help us move forward. Without this information, there's a risk we are unable to move on.

Dave remembers learning from uncomfortable feedback while in a job managing a leadership team. He thought of himself as open to new ideas, and spent time encouraging team discussions to generate new ideas to be acted on. Sometimes he felt the other team members could be suggesting more ideas of their own but he wasn't sure how to get there.

He received feedback from a team member during a regular performance review, which opened his eyes to the brutal facts. He was told "In our team meetings we all know which of the alternative ideas will be chosen by you, Dave, because they will be the ideas you personally suggested. We've learned it's not worth us pitching many ideas of our own, because you don't choose them."

Ouch! Dave wasn't aware he was suppressing other ideas in favour of his own, so he kept an eye on this and discovered it was often true. While he felt uncomfortable receiving the feedback, he says he regulated that feeling by repeatedly telling himself, silently, "It's good to improve and I needed to learn". The feedback catalysed a simple switch in his behaviour which resulted in lots more ideas being generated by his team. Many of their ideas he described as being much better than his own!

Within three months of making these changes, Dave found himself being invited to facilitate ideation events and then to lead a large innovation project. The direct and specific feedback he received and acted on was the key to unlocking many new opportunities for him. Remember to ask for feedback yourself and be prepared to learn from it.

To learn the most from feedback you must make sure there is some level of precision in it, so you know exactly what steps you've done well, and exactly what you'd need to do to fill a gap successfully.

To illustrate precise feedback here are some real examples from our clients. You'll notice some contain more precision than others and the better the precision, the more helpful the feedback.

Feedback phrases which point to a strength

"Liu, when you work in a team, your relationship skills mean the team work well together and deliver their service accurately and cheerfully."

> The precision level is good: it's about being in a team, good relationship skills and the impact of those skills in the team. To learn more we can ask "How could my relationship skills be used more outside of my work in a team?"

"Shen, do what you usually do and get this activity to speed up so we meet the deadline."

> This is vague feedback. To push for more precision we can ask "What is it I 'usually do' which you feel will help most?" We add the word "most" to encourage even more value into the reply.

"Shen, I've called you because I need someone who can dig deep into this problem and find the real cause of it."

> This has a medium level of precision: the feedback highlights the ability to dig into a situation. To be clearer we can ask: "What do you mean by dig deep and what is the problem?"

Feedback phrases about gaps

"Kelvin, the report conclusion needs to include the evidence you used to reach the conclusion."

> A good level of precision directing attention to exactly where the improvement is needed.

"Kelvin, your presentation was good for experts but your audience are all beginners and need a step-by-step approach."

> A medium level of precision. To learn more we can ask "What size of steps would be right, for next time?"

"Kelvin, your throughput in the office will improve if you just do what everyone else does."

> This is poor feedback because the vagueness leaves us wondering what it is everyone else does, which will improve throughput. It also lacks any measures describing the current throughput and the expected target.

Later in this chapter you will discover how to learn more from the short pieces of feedback you receive 'in the moment', how to filter feedback, and how to change the way you ask for feedback when you feel someone is uncomfortable in discussing gaps with you.

Warning: If feedback is always "you'll be ready-later"

A project leader described his situation to us:

> "I was being given feedback that I'd be ready for the senior project role in 18 months to 2 years. I'd heard the same message for four years in a row. It eventually dawned on me something needed to change and I was going to have to drive a change myself. I asked for more specific feedback about the gaps in my skills and experience and took steps to fill the gaps. A year later the message was still the same. 18 months to 2 years away. I started to ask more about what was between me and getting the senior role. Eventually I understood. The senior roles were filled, and there was nothing planned to create new vacancies. The message hit home. I needed to change organisation to achieve the role I wanted."

If your feedback, year after year, says you are still eighteen months to two years away from being ready-now then it is time to have a brutal-facts conversation with your manager and stakeholders. If the conversation gives you messages about gaps you need to fill in your competencies, then the following sections will help you. If the conversation reveals competencies are not the issue then you may need to make a bigger change, like the project manager in our example.

Manager's Note: In Part II, the managers' section, learn more about feedback on page 201, and on page 257.

Learning more from 'in-the-moment' feedback

Our advice whenever you're given feedback is always to ask an open question to help you understand more, and to help you to decide what to do with the feedback. Use this approach when you're formally asking for feedback, and especially when you unexpectedly receive spontaneous feedback 'in-the-moment'.

The following are examples of 'in-the-moment' feedback phrases you may hear, which lack precision. They are all about gaps. Below each are several questions which you can ask to understand more and to decide what to do, if anything:

Feedback: "You have spent too much."
Ask: "What's the implication of spending too much?"
"How much money was available?"
"How can I find out how much is available next time?"
"How much overspend can be accommodated in future?"

Feedback: "Not everyone enjoyed the entire presentation."
Ask: "Who said they enjoyed it and who said they didn't?"
"Which parts of the presentation were enjoyed?"
"What has been the effect of not everyone enjoying it all?"
"How well has the presentation met its objectives?"

Feedback: "You need to work harder."
Ask: "What needs to improve as a result of me working harder?"
"What are good ways to show I'm working harder?"
"Which parts of my work are going OK?"

Feedback: "Your report is lacking and needs re-writing."
Ask: "Which sections are ok, and which should change?"
"What haven't I said that's important to say?"
"Who could mentor or coach me to help me improve it?"

Feedback: "John hasn't said a good word about you."
Ask: "What has John actually said?"
"What change does John need to see?"
"Who do you hear saying better things about me?"

Build on the approach in these examples to develop your own open, precision questions to drive out more value from the in-the-moment feedback you receive.

A helpful way to think about feedback

A psychologist we've worked with explained to us how she deals with the feedback she receives. We use her approach ourselves. Here's how she describes it:

"I treat all feedback as a gift. I imagine I have a small feedback sack hanging from my belt. When I get feedback, good or not good, I thank the giver and I mentally pop their feedback into the bag and let it sit there for a day or so. If the feedback includes some dissatisfaction I don't shoot the messenger or argue with them.

A couple of days later, I'll take the feedback out and decide what to do with it. Some will have been given in an unhelpful way but the time-out allows me to see the gems without being distracted by how they were delivered. I may decide to act on some feedback immediately, remembering to smile to myself about the good feedback, even writing it down to use in my performance review. For others, I will plan to approach things differently next time a situation occurs.

Some feedback I'll decide not to do anything about; perhaps because you can't please all the people all of the time, or because when compared to other feedback I've received I decide I'm just going to let it go. And that's important too. To move on and let it go."

When you receive feedback, use a similar approach by accepting it as a gift, allowing it to settle for a short time, and then deciding how you'll act on it.

"There's no learning without having lots of ideas and failing lots of times."
Sir Jony Ive, Apple's senior vice president of design

When you are asked to collect feedback

In your existing role, or as you prepare for the next, your manger may suggest you collect feedback. They may even suggest a number of people you should ask for the feedback.

Before you start, here's how to make this activity a more productive and useful exercise, reducing the risk you receive a range of unstructured feedback.

- Understand the reason for getting feedback. Talk to your manager, or the person making the suggestion, and agree the outcome of seeking feedback. Use the following questions as prompts:

- What are you seeking feedback about? Is it a particular piece of work, the impression you create in a team, specific behaviours and how they are interpreted by others, or something else?

- What is the purpose behind seeking feedback? Is it to inform a development plan, to help make your day-to-day work more effective, or for some other reason?

▪ Work out who you want to ask for feedback. Choose people who have knowledge of the activities, skills or behaviours which are relevant. Remember seeking feedback can be used a part of an influencing strategy, to increase your visibility, and to place your performance into the thoughts of a decision-maker. Use these opportunities to decide who you will ask.

▪ Prepare the person you want feedback from. Let them know what you want the feedback about, what you'll be using it for, and how you would like to receive the feedback. Opt for a face to face discussion, or a phone call, if possible, as it gives you the opportunity to clarify any imprecise feedback comments. You can even give the person a set of structured questions which will help to focus their thinking and encourage them to explain with specific examples.

If the feedback you receive doesn't match your own view it maybe they are seeing something you are not. We all have our blind spots! However, it may also be that the feedback they are giving you is not accurate for some reason.

In these cases, it can help to get feedback from a number of sources and then look for consistent messages or themes. Ask yourself:

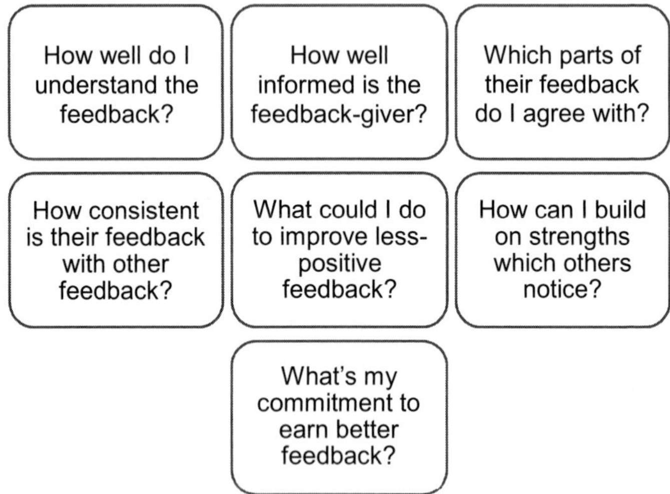

How well do I understand the feedback?
How well informed is the feedback-giver?
Which parts of their feedback do I agree with?
How consistent is their feedback with other feedback?
What could I do to improve less-positive feedback?
How can I build on strengths which others notice?
What's my commitment to earn better feedback?

How to overcome reluctant feedback-giving

Now you're well prepared for receiving feedback constructively, your job is to encourage others to give you that feedback. You'll find some feedback givers will launch immediately into a mix of your strengths and gaps feedback. A feedback-giver from Neil's experience, however, plunged directly into describing just his gaps, and explained "I'm not here to spend time giving you good feedback."

That's a solid reminder to get feedback from a number of different sources!

Some potential feedback-givers will need extra encouragement to help them feel comfortable giving gap-feedback which could help you improve. They worry they may offend someone and damage a relationship. When you encounter feedback which ends with "... I can't think of any gaps ..." it could mean that everything is fine (time to celebrate) or it could indicate you need to ask for feedback in a way which sounds easier to answer.

Asking "What could I do differently" is a good way of asking the gaps question from another angle. Doing something differently doesn't sound good or bad, it's just a choice. This question will step up the value you get from your feedback givers.

Getting the most value out of feedback you receive is a perfect topic to discuss with a coach rather than a mentor. The coach can keep the discussion positive and ask you questions which will help you create a plan of action to take you closer towards your goal.

"Feedback is the breakfast of champions"
Ken Blanchard

Chapter review

Take steps to acquire feedback regularly and challenge yourself to make 'regularly' mean more often than it does now. Manage your immediate reaction to feedback and decide carefully what actions to take for a positive outcome. This is a productive way of tuning your performance to match or exceed what's expected of you.

Use what you've learned in this chapter to guide your response when someone asks you for feedback on their performance too.

Reflect on what you've discovered about feedback by asking yourself the following questions. This will, again, help you make your ideas and decisions clearer and strengthen your learning.

Collecting and learning from feedback

- Who will you seek feedback from?
- What do you want feedback on?
- How will you respond to feedback differently now independent of whether it's positive or not?
- What will you do to remind yourself to ask for feedback more regularly?
- How will you *give* feedback differently, now you've read this chapter?

7

Portable soft skills

You will have heard 'soft skills' are important when finding a role and delivering a role but they are often shrouded in mystery.

In this section, we'll explore what we mean by soft skills, and the reason managers are increasingly making hiring decisions based upon them.

Soft skills are the behaviours we use at work and in life. For example, we may have good listening skills and problem solving skills. We may be able to develop a human connection with other people quickly. We may be able to disagree without harming a relationship. We may be able to set expectations in a way that helps people around us feel motivated in a good way, and able to recognise their success. We may be able to create a plan to help ourselves and others deliver the success we need at the time we need it. We may know how to collaborate in a team and communicate our ideas effectively. We may have adaptability, being able to decide when staying the same is essential, and when making some changes will work better. We may be good at making decisions which meet the often-conflicting demands of time, quality and cost.

Often it's specialist skills which will get you an interview while soft skills get you the job and help you keep it. For some jobs, however, if will be your softs skills which get you the interview.

In 2015, James Caan CBE, businessman and entrepreneur, co-led a consultation to understand how to encourage individuals to value their soft skills more. Research conducted for the consultation, reported in Forbes, found that 97% of employers describe soft skills as directly contributing to the success of their businesses and over half said that soft skills are more important than academic results. The research also uncovered that while four out of five staff feel confident in describing their soft skills, 54% forget to mention their soft skills on their CV and in job applications.

So, develop your soft skills, recognise you have them and remember to talk about them too.

Four secrets about portable soft skills

Knowing these four secrets places you ahead of the competition. While the secrets themselves will seem like common sense, they are not always common practice. And that's where you can develop your advantage.

Secret One: Not everyone is aware that soft skills may make the difference between you getting a role, and someone else getting the role. Increasingly the hiring managers are looking beyond the specialist knowledge and have expectations about *how* they would like a role to be delivered.

Here are common examples of soft skills. Below each, are a selection of tools and behaviours which contribute to demonstrating the soft skill, and which you can learn more about in this book.

Listening effectively and being open to new ideas

- Listening
- Precision Questions
- Flexibility

Curious and comfortable with not knowing all the answers

- Open questions
- Listening
- Self-talk

Planning ahead, doing what's important

- Clear purpose
- Towards approach
- Flexibility

Ethically influencing to reach a good outcome for all

- Listening
- Flexible Communication
- Common purpose
- Good attitude

Asking tough questions while keeping good relationships

- Signaling intent
- Open questions
- Precision questions
- Listening

Asking questions to find out details or understand purpose

- Open questions
- Precision questions
- Questions to find the bigger picture

Being self-motivated and motivating others

- FLOW
- Towards approach
- Giving feedback
- Communication skills

Working well in a team

- Communication skills
- Towards approach
- Flexibility
- Open Questions
- Precision
- Listening
- Common purpose

Remaining goals focused despite distractions & set-backs

- Persistence
- Self-talk
- Flexibility
- Helpful ways to process feedback

Able to make a decision in situations of uncertainty

- Towards approach
- Improve decision-making

Able to delegate effectively

- Towards approach
- Creating Strong outcomes
- Open questions
- Precision Questions

Secret Two: Soft skills are highly portable. A soft skill you have developed in one role can be sought after in very different roles, and across different organisations.

This means strong soft skills can help you get a very different role to the one you have now, or help you get a related role in another industry.

Secret Three: You can develop soft skills just like you can develop specialist or technical skills. In the chapters about preparing to fill the gaps and filling the gaps you'll find out how to develop the approaches and behaviours which contribute to strengthening these soft skills.

Secret Four: As your role becomes more senior and more influential you will use more of the soft skills and use less of your specialist skills.

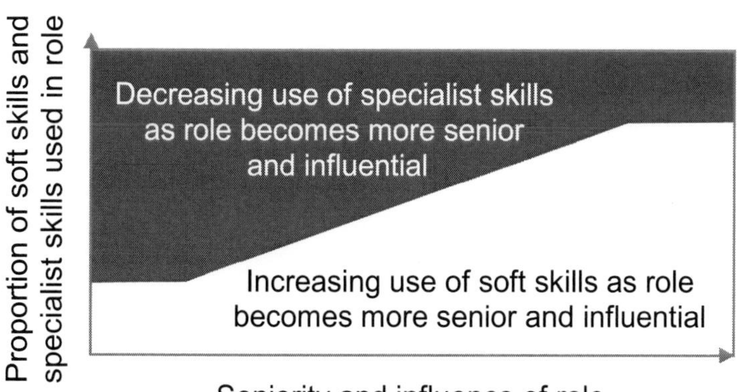

Take a moment to note how strongly you use each of the soft skills listed in Secret One, compared to how strongly you may need to use them in your next role.

A Refreshing Role Change

Soft skills can be the spring-board which helps you change roles to something quite different.

After a colleague, Oliver, sat down and reviewed what role he wanted to do next, and noted his strengths and gaps, he had a discussion with his manager. He explained what he noticed during the conversation:

> "It was quickly apparent to me there were not going to be any vacancies in the near future which appealed to me and brought me new challenges. Not within my current organisation anyway.
>
> My manager was doing his best to create options but realistically they were 'more of the same' for me. It was time to bite the bullet. I'd enjoyed strengthening my portable soft skills recently so I applied for a role where my knowledge of the technical area was very limited but where the key was working with different characters, consulting technical experts, building good relationships and trust and gradually influence decision-makers. Exactly matching the soft skills I'd been strengthening.
>
> I got the job!
>
> There are lots of experts around me who have the technical skills, but that's ok because my soft skills are helping me build good relationships with them, and they look happy when I ask them for advice. Interestingly, when I ask questions to get the advice, the conversations often surface new ideas because no-one has asked the naïve questions for a while!"

So, remember the power of soft skills and, if it is right for you, use them as a springboard to a refreshing change.

|| Pause Here: New Opportunities using skills you already have

Just before you jump into the world of 'filling the gaps', we encourage you to take a short pause here. You've spent time deciding what you want in a role and you've been honest with yourself about your strengths and the gaps you'll need to fill. And you're prepared to work on them too. Before you go any further, ask yourself these questions:

- What new opportunities could exist for me based simply on my existing, established strengths?

- Now I know more about what I want to do, what opportunities are there to do more of it in my existing role? What's stopping me?

Frequently we coach individuals who suddenly realise they could be using their strengths more broadly in their existing role and enjoying what they already have. They just hadn't been clear about what they wanted to do and what would make them happy. They hadn't been able to ask for what they wanted. It may be unrealistic to assume we can influence how we do every job, but test that assumption before you make it. You may get a pleasant surprise.

Chapter review

Now you know the role you want, and you have the tools to tell others what you want and to ask for their help. You also understand your strengths and gaps.

This is an important milestone, so reflect on what you have discovered by asking yourself the following questions, based on what you've read in this chapter. This will, again, help you make your ideas and decisions clearer and strengthen your learning.

Portable soft skills

- Which soft skills do you feel will be important for you?
- Which soft skills are already a strength for you?
- Which soft skill will you make it a priority to improve?
- What else could you do with the skills and knowledge you have now? What does that change for you?

From reading the previous chapters, you'll now be aware of how to describe the role you want and tell others; how to ask for help in achieving your next role; and how to describe your strengths and gaps and use feedback. You'll be aware of how your skills compare to the essentials of your next role; the benefits of portable skills and how your existing skills may lead to more in your current role, or provide a springboard to a refreshing change

You're now set to take action and prepare yourself to fill the important gaps to become ready-now. Do this while thinking about the role you want next and also keep in mind ideas about what you might want to do further in the future.

8

Preparing to fill the gaps

You now have an idea of what role you want and you know how the needs of the role compare with your own strengths and gaps. How do you close the gaps? Well, read on and you'll find simple tools and techniques you can use to make the changes you need.

But first, prepare yourself with the tips in this chapter which will help you approach your gaps in a manageable way.

Extract the most from your current job

As we coach clients who are preparing for their next role, they describe the new skills and experience they need. When we ask how they could obtain these, they frequently discover that they could have been practising many of them in their existing role, and have missed that opportunity.

Whether you are in the early stages of your job, or well established, you may have noticed someone doing a job which feels like the next step for you on your career path. Ask a few questions to learn more about the key skills, knowledge and behaviours needed for that next step. Then gradually make opportunities for yourself to learn and practise them a little while you are delivering your current role. Your learning will give you an early advantage in gaining the critical capabilities for your next role, plus you'll have started to draw attention to where your ambitions lie. Of course, you'll also have more opportunities to decide whether that next-step role is right for you.

Approaching the gaps : Keep motivated

As you begin to fill the gaps, use an understanding of FLOW to increase your motivation and success. Use FLOW to manage your motivation when you are in your new role too.

A client, John, told us his story about how he learned of FLOW after he applied successfully for a promotion as a project manager:

"I'd been a member of many project teams and felt eager to lead a team of my own, as a project manager. By the end of the first week in the job, I was highly stressed and felt paralysed: Stakeholders were expecting reports from me. The objective of the project felt like a huge challenge. I hadn't got a team and I could feel time ticking by.

When I talked to my mentor she showed me the FLOW picture and how we can feel motivated, 'pleasantly stressed' and 'in the zone' when the size of the challenge is balanced by our perception of our capability to tackle the challenge.

At that moment, the size of the challenge felt massive to me and my capability felt very low. We talked about breaking the project down into manageable stages and then about who could help by being on the team for the first stage. Suddenly I could talk about my next steps and my energy was back. It's a fantastic tool. I keep a copy of it on my wall. It reminds me to regularly talk to the team about the next stage, the challenges of that stage and what capabilities we'll need to succeed."

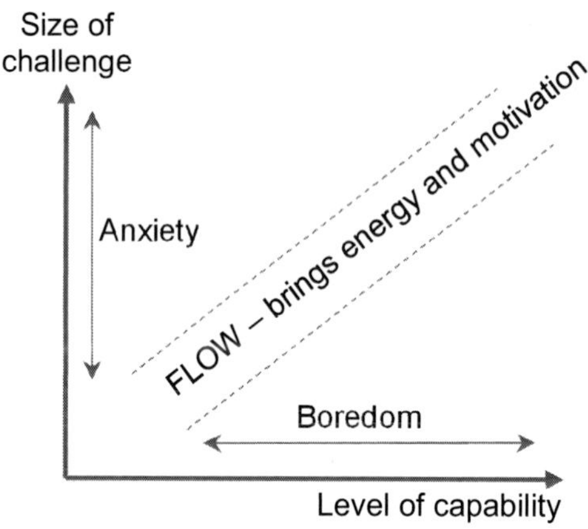

FLOW – Achieved by balancing challenge and capability

FLOW is a feeling of involvement and energised focus. We achieve our best performance when in FLOW. This is true whether we are working on our own or as a part of a team.

Perhaps you've experienced FLOW for yourself while doing something you enjoy. For example, working on a hobby activity; planning to spend an hour on it and suddenly finding three hours have gone by without you noticing!

FLOW: In good balance = good motivation

Flow occurs when there is a good, sustained balance between

a) the size of the challenge you are working on

b) your perception of your capability to do the work

(capability = having the skills & resources personally, or having them available to you)

FLOW: Out of balance = bad stress and anxiety

If the challenge feels too high compared to your capability to achieve it, you will become anxious and stressed. FLOW will not occur and your performance will reduce. To get back into balance ask yourself; How can the challenge can be broken down into stages? What are the steps needed to achieve the first stage? Who can help me with advice, skills or resources?

A client, Nicky, passed on the following reflection on the level of FLOW in her new role:

> "New roles are supposed to be stretching. The size of the challenge needs to be activating rather than suppressing. When I started this new role, it was helpful to talk to my boss about breaking-up the challenge into several stages, which I would use to get myself up to speed. We both understood the stages and, although each was still a challenge, I knew I hadn't got to learn it all in one go and that helped reduce the stress for me and kept me motivated."

Out of balance – causing boredom

If your capability is high compared with the size of the challenge you are working on, you'll become bored. Again, FLOW will not occur, and your performance will reduce.

The reason Nicky left her previous role was because of this low level of challenge. She explained:

> "I was honest with myself. I was doing my job with less and less of my mental capacity. I asked myself 'is this ok, or is this telling me it's time for a new challenge?' I knew adding more volume of the same work would have raised the challenge and helped me back into FLOW but I decided more of the same wouldn't motivate me in the right way, so I took a new job."

When you start to address your gaps, and later when you step into your new role with the expectation of a challenge, be prepared with your strategies for getting motivated by being in FLOW:

- Recognise when there is a good balance of challenge and capability and take steps to maintain it. Often, we are motivated by a challenge that seems a little bit beyond our capabilities, but within a reachable distance.
- Recognise when there is a lack of balance. Decide how larger challenges can be broken into smaller stages. Find out where you can get help. Decide what you will do first.
- If appropriate, discuss staged expectations with your manager.
- Consider getting coached on the subject of achieving and maintaining FLOW in what you do.

Fine-tuning how you learn, to learn more effectively

Being prepared for your next role will invariably involve some learning. To make the most of your time, and learn efficiently, you'll need to understand the key steps involved in effective learning and how to tune your approach so it matches you own preferences.

We recommend a well-known, four stage learning cycle which creates effective learning. Shown below, the Kolb learning cycle is named after the educational theorist who developed it.

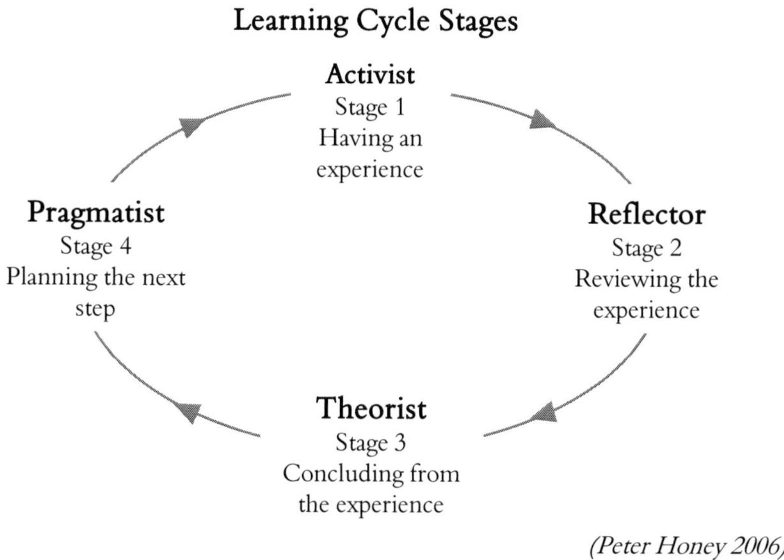

(Peter Honey 2006)

As an example of this cycle's application, imagine you are on holiday and notice the hotel offers a scuba diving experience. You love new experiences so you take the following approach.

Stage 1 - You go for a first trial dive with an instructor who looks after all of the technical and safety steps. You experience swimming underwater and see plenty of beautiful fish and corals.

Stage 2 - After the event you get back onto dry land and reflect on what a great time you had. Maybe you even look through the photos you took on your underwater camera and revisit the sights. You describe the experience to your friends and family.

Stage 3 – You reach the conclusion you so enjoyed the experience of diving, you want to do more of it. You decide you will become a qualified diver.

Stage 4 - You create your plan of how to become qualified, which involves joining a local scuba club and learning with them.

You then continue with the cycle, starting again at Stage 1:

Stage 1 – You attend your first scuba club night…and so on, through the cycle of stages again.

It's easy to see how this cycle can be applied to other learning situations and also that you can enter the cycle at any of the stages. As individuals, we all have stages we prefer to linger over, or use to enter the cycle. There's no right or wrong place to start. In the example above, we could have started with a conclusion to learn to scuba dive (Stage 3) and followed on from there. It's just important to use all the stages.

If you miss stages out of the learning cycle, then your learning will be incomplete. You may have experienced this. For example, some people rush from one activity to the next without taking any time to reflect on what happened or to draw any conclusions. They repeatedly make the same mistakes and get frustrated with themselves, or create frustration around them.

Another common example of incomplete learning is '*analysis paralysis.*' You'll observe this when someone spends all of their time reflecting, or concluding from their past experience, but never move into constructing their plan or acting on their learning. They don't turn thought into action.

Both of these examples highlight that a good way to optimise your learning is to complete all the steps in the cycle.

An extra way of optimising your learning is to recognise which stage in the cycle you prefer the most. We each have our own preferences, and it's good to start your learning with your favourite step; making sure, though, that you move on around the cycle.

Your personal preference may be clear to you already: Perhaps you've completed a learning styles questionnaire or perhaps you've noticed some methods of learning just don't appeal to you.

A friend, Jacob, told us how he discovered what didn't work for him.

"My manager asked me to learn about a new engine and give me several of his own books to read and digest. I kept meaning to read the books but never got around to it. They just sat on the shelf. Eventually the guy I work with asked if I'd like to help strip down the new engine. I was there like a shot. Jumping in was my way of starting to learn, not reading books."

Learning by jumping in suited Jacob, but you may be someone for whom the words 'jumping in' hold a particular horror. How could you possibly jump into something without understanding the background and theory? These are examples of learning preferences showing themselves.

We regularly hear about a mismatch occurring between the learning preference of a manager and their employee.

While listening to an explanation of learning styles during a training course, two of the attendees exchanged a glance across the room. They explained one of them was a manager and the other their employee, and they'd just realised why there had been no progress in achieving the employee's development plan. The manager had written the plan, and written it for their own preference which was to jump in and have a go. He had given his employee the opportunity to create a small project so they could begin to experience project management.

The employee had good intentions, and regarded personal development as very important, but had never managed to get around to starting the project. They wanted the project they chose to be valuable, and needed to feel prepared with some project management skills before starting.

The manager subsequently created a joint development plan with the employee helping to choose a valuable project goal and a useful project management beginners' course. The employee found this approach much more to their liking and good progress was made. The manager then provided more help by ensuring her employee had time to draw conclusions, plan the next step, and launch the project.

It often helps to work with someone who has a learning preference different from your own because they will ask questions or suggest activities you would not have considered. This will help to motivate you to complete the cycle.

Now you understand the power of the learning cycle, reflect for a moment on the following questions, draw your conclusions, plan what you'll do differently, and take action.

- How do you prefer to learn?
- How can you use that knowledge to help you in starting your learning?
- What help do you need to make sure you complete the full learning cycle?

Have a towards approach

We've described before how someone wanting to change their career can often easily describe what they dislike in their current situation, or what they don't want. This is the 'away from' approach. While it can be useful to know what you don't want, if it is your only strategy you may find yourself in a new role which still doesn't meet all your needs.

To progress, you will find it far more valuable to have a 'towards' approach. By knowing what outcome you want, you can evaluate the options available to you and choose one which moves you in the right direction.

As you make a note of the outcomes you want, apply these quick rules to make them strong outcomes:

- The outcome should be stated in the positive rather than the negative; what you want rather than what you don't.

- Psychologists tell us the outcome should be described in the past tense (as though it's already happened) and describing what the outcome looks like, sounds like, feels like or how another person might describe it. For example: "My outcome is that by the end of this year I will have become a successful author with my book visible on major booksellers' shelves and transcribed into audio tapes in five languages. My high school will have written about 'how proud' they were to hear of my achievement."

- The outcome should be possible, achievable, and stretching. For instance, it's possible for someone born a UK citizen to become prime minister of the UK, but not for them to become President of the USA.

- The resources required to achieve the outcome must be either immediately available or accessible.

- It must have a defined time frame. ('one day I want to be...' is not a defined time frame, 'in ten years' time' is)

- It should be consistent with your core values and what you want to achieve in your life as a whole.

It may not be a single step to get from A to B, to achieve your outcomes, yet every step you take will be in the direction which move you towards your eventual goal.

Connecting the role to your purpose

As you look at a potential new role, decide how it would fit with your purpose in life. When we talk to clients who are unhappy in their role, there is often a mismatch between what they are doing and their purpose.

In its simplest form, discovering the link between the role and our purpose is achieved by repeatedly asking the question "And when I have that, what will it give me?" This approach moves your thinking from the specific to the more general, from the detail to the bigger picture. It's the opposite of asking precision questions and helps you decide how a step you wish to take helps (or doesn't help) you to reach your goals and purpose. An example is shown next.

Note: Read this example from bottom to top as it illustrates a person making the connection between their plan for a new role, and their own happiness.

Happiness - I'm meeting my core values

↑

And when I have that what will it give me?

↑

Facts to lobby a better deal for developing countries

↑

And when I have that what will it give me?

↑

Understanding of how to work across cultures

↑

And when I have that what will it give me?

↑

I'll visit developing countries observing their cultures

↑

And when I have that what will it give me?

↑

I'm going to take on a role with international travel

Once you reach 'happiness' you've probably reached the point where you are connecting with part of your purpose in life.

This is a good check to do when you're deciding on the suitability of a new role. It can reveal some interesting implications of taking of taking on a new role, and may spark new ideas about how to get to each level. Making the connection between a role and your purpose is also a good way of giving your motivation a boost. We feel more motivated when we are doing something which fits with our purpose in life.

If you ask yourself the question 'And when I have that, what will it give me?' and discover the answers are not taking you towards your purpose, then either think again about the role, or decide what actions you'll take to make the answers fit.

If the previous example had started as 'I'm going to take on a role with international travel', and finished with 'I'll spend a lot of time away when I really want to be with my family' it would encourage a decision between selecting a different role, or deciding how you would make being away from your family become acceptable.

Making the connection between an activity and the underlying purpose is a helpful tool in many day-to-day situations. In meetings where the conversation is becoming lost in the detail, asking the question "when we've decided this, what will it give us?" is a powerful way of hopping over the immediate detail and concentrating on the bigger picture purpose again. We can check to make sure the purpose is still clear, and to check what other ways there might be of achieving it.

When you're struggling to find the enthusiasm to do an activity, ask yourself the question "when I've done this, what will it give me" several times. You will connect the activity with a bigger purpose, and that connection creates energy and motivation.

Identifying risks and preparing for them

Each new role will bring a collection of potential benefits for you. Making the most of these benefits is a must, so take a moment to reflect on what risks may emerge from taking the role, so you can take care of the risks and reap all of the benefits.

A new role will introduce change to your life and you can learn from the world of project management how to manage the risks and implications associated with a change.

In any project, the team identify the risks which might get in the way of the project achieving its goal. They decide how they will either remove the risks or mitigate them, handling them safely and reducing their impact if they do occur. So, what kind of risks are we talking about in the context of a role change? In the table below are some risk and implication examples, followed by how they may be removed or mitigated.

Risk or Implication Title	Impact	Mitigation
Risk: I may need to move location with the new job at some time in the future	Children's schools change with the surprise causing unhappy children	Negotiate 12-month warning of a location change. Talk to children about the move when facts are available. Involve children in choice of school. Visit to make new friends before move
Implication: Part time work means a reduction in salary	Less money available to spend on holidays	Create a new budget for holidays and book new holidays to meet budget

Risk: My promotion to manage the team I work in may cause resentment from co-workers	Poor relationships in the team and a risk of poorer performance	Develop approach to manage the change of relationship. Seek advice from a peer who has experienced a similar change in this organisation
Implication: New role is isolated. I will no longer be part of a team	I could feel left out and will miss the ability to discuss things within the team	Maintain plenty of existing relationships on an informal basis and discuss what I can. Use a personal coach to support me with the transition & confidential issues

These examples illustrate the difference between a risk: something which might happen as a consequence of taking a specific role, and an implication: something which will happen.

The actual risks and implications will be specific to you as an individual. Take the time to decide what they might be and how to manage them. Your approach doesn't need to be as formal as creating a risk chart. It's the thinking which delivers the benefits.

You'll benefit from talking this through with a coach, a mentor or another third party who has a different learning style to your own. They may identify risks you've not seen. Discussing a role's benefits, risks and implications can also be a useful way of organising a discussion with partners or family. The approach can ensure you've heard their opinions and ideas, so the right steps are taken to make the change a success.

Chapter review

Before you start to fill the gaps, take the time to reflect on what you've discovered by asking yourself the following questions, based on what you've read in this chapter.

Preparing to fill the gaps

- What could you be practising in your current role to help prepare you for the next?
- What encourages FLOW for you, and what interrupts it?
- What is your preferred learning style?
- How will you use this knowledge to ensure you learn effectively?
- Who can help make sure you complete the entire learning cycle?
- What are you moving towards?
- How does your next role align with your purpose?
- What are the key risks you face?
- What are you doing to mitigate these risks?

9

Filling the gaps

Now you've prepared yourself for effectively addressing the gaps so that you can become ready-now. From our conversations with clients, consultants, and from our own experience, we have added the solutions to the gaps which occur for many job holders and job seekers. Decide which are the most relevant to you and take action.

10

Gap: I need to listen and communicate better

Whenever we meet somebody either for the first time, or even if we've known them for a period of time, it helps our communication when we establish a level of rapport with them. Rapport can be defined as having a good understanding of someone and an ability to communicate well with them. You may have met people you're quickly comfortable being with and enjoy talking to. You and they will have had a high degree of rapport. You may also remember situations where you have found someone abrasive or difficult. In those situations, you'll have had a low level of rapport.

Throughout the process of moving from one job role to another, there are many occasions where it's useful or even vital to establish a level of rapport with another person. For example, having a chat to find out about a role, an informal interview, an assessment centre or a formal interview. People tend to help people they like. One of the reasons we like people is their ability to establish rapport with us. Once rapport has been created, everything seems to go more easily.

Of course, the skills of listening and communicating well are valuable outside the workplace in personal relationships and beyond.

The following sections describe how to build good rapport, how to listen more effectively and how to tune your communications to get the best effect.

Building rapport with good listening skills

It is highly unlikely anyone will feel a degree of rapport with you if they don't believe you're listening to them. If you imagine a situation in which you don't believe you are being listened to, what emotion does it create in you? For some, the answer will be frustration, others, annoyance or upset or even anger. These are not the positive emotions we want other people to associate with us when we want to build a relationship with them.

So, what behaviours will give someone the clue you are not listening with full attention?

Review the following list of poor-listening behaviours and check which of the behaviours someone might catch you displaying.

Poor Listening Behaviours

- Giving no eye contact (looks out of the window)
- Doesn't give full attention (greets passers-by, checks emails while 'listening')
- Continuing with task (uses laptop when 'listening')
- Time watching
- No acknowledgement of speaker (no nods or verbal acknowledgements)
- Monosyllabic comments, unenthusiastic
- Changing the subject
- Dishonest – doesn't say "I've no time now, can we arrange an alternative time?"

Avoid these and instead stick to the behaviours on this next list. They are very effective not only in communicating you're listening but, when you use them, you'll hear and remember more too.

Good listening behaviours

- Give balanced eye contact (avoid continuously staring)
- Turn towards the speaker
- Look at speaker
- Give affirmation – saying "Yes", "Ok", nodding
- Ask questions for clarification, staying on the topic
- Paraphrase to check your understanding ("What I understand so far is …")
- Respond honestly and positively

Pause for a moment to answer the following questions.

- Who do you regard as a good listener?
- How do you feel about them?
- Which behaviours do they demonstrate from the good listening behaviours list?
- What does this tell you about the behaviours you need to demonstrate as you interact with people not only in discussions about your career but also more broadly in life?

Building rapport using awareness of communication styles

When you've experienced communicating with someone but the connection just doesn't seem to work well, this is often because you both have different preference for the styles of communication you use most.

People tend to like people who are like themselves – in the early stages of a relationship anyway. We communicate most easily with people who communicate in a similar style to us. In its simplest form, communication preferences work almost like a language. We can easily imagine how unintended results can emerge from two people talking to each other while using different languages.

A simple way of identifying different communication styles is based on how much we use an 'asking' style or a 'telling' style, and whether we use a larger or smaller amount of emotion in our communication.

The following figure illustrates how these preferences characterise four communications styles.

The four communication styles

Communicate with low emotion

Asking style of communication

Analytic style	Driving style
Amiable style	Expressive style

Telling style of communication

Communicate with high emotion

Everyone has their own preference for how much 'asking' or 'telling' they use in their communication, and also how much emotion they prefer. Those who prefer low emotion and a telling style are referred to as having a Driving preference. They're often seen as people who control their emotions and speak assertively. They prefer to take charge and are focused on big-picture results. They are often regarded by others as highly efficient and not concerned about relationships or feelings.

Those who have a preference for a telling style and also a degree of emotion are said to have an Expressive preference. They show their emotions and speak assertively. They enjoy sharing their ideas and perspectives openly with others. Others may see them as creative, but a bit unfocused.

Those with a more asking preference and who communicate with a degree of emotion have an Amiable preference. They share their emotions openly and prefer to ask questions rather than give orders. Relationships, feelings and personal security are important to them. Others may see them as warm and talkative with less interest in facts.

The final grouping is those who use an asking preference with lower emotion. These have an Analytic preference. They control their emotions and tend to ask questions rather than give orders. They have a high degree of focus and enjoy accuracy and act deliberately to achieve that end. Others may see them as slow-paced and detail-oriented.

As you reflect on these preferences start to identify your own communication preference and the preferences of others around you, including those you've had difficulty communicating with in the past. Use the previous figure to help.

During a workshop, Nicole highlighted for us how different communications style preferences can block good communications:

> "I realise now how I made a bad start when I met my boss for the first time. I've got an Amiable preference and went to talk to him. He's definitely got a Driving preference. To me, relationships and emotions are very important so I told him all about my weekend, the highs and the lows, and asked him lots of questions about his weekend too. He started to look a bit frustrated so I shared some more about how I enjoyed my previous jobs, just so he could know me better. Suddenly he interrupted and said 'Right, enough of that, let's talk about the sales results.'"

> "I felt we'd had a bad start and didn't know why. I realise now that those with a Driving preference can find the relationship building conversation less important. Just 'chit chat'. A bit of a waste of time because they have less of an interest in the relationships, preferring to get on with the job at hand."

So how can you use this knowledge to help you communicate more effectively?

The good news is we're talking about preferences, and not about unchangeable patterns. It's just a matter of practice to increase your flexibility in using different communications styles. Here are the four steps you can take. Clues to help you answer the questions in steps 1 and 2 can be found immediately after the list of steps.

First, notice if the person you want to talk with has a communication style which is different from yours. If the styles are very similar, no action is necessary. If they are different, continue with the steps below.

1. Notice if they 'ask' more than you or 'tell' more than you
2. Notice if they use more or less emotion in their communication than you
3. Sprinkle a bit more of their style into your communication (i.e. increase or decrease your 'asking' or 'telling' and adjust your use of emotion). They'll find this more natural for them and your conversations will be easier as a result

Here are the clues to help you identify 'asking' behaviours:

Asking behaviours

- Rarely uses physical gestures
- Rarely uses firm voice tone to emphasise
- More cooperative and patient
- Give less eye contact. Gentle handshake
- Often use qualified language *("it's fine, as long as x and y continue working")*
- Often quiet in group situations
- Slower to introduce themselves
- Keep many of their opinions to themselves

And now the clues to 'telling' behaviours:

Telling behaviours

- Physical gestures are common
- Frequent use of firm voice tone to emphasise points
- More competitive
- Eye contact is strong. Firm handshake
- Have limited patience
- Sound certain, decisive and are happy to share their opinions with others
- Likely to introduce themselves quickly
- Confident to speak out in a group

Clues to communicating with low emotion:

Low emotion communication

- Keep their feelings to themselves
- Use a smaller set of facial expressions
- Noticing their emotions can be more difficult
- Use a more formal style
- Don't seek physical contact as often
- Follow structure, for example, an agenda
- Talk about specific details and are clear about facts
- Keep conversations on-topic

Finally, clues to communicating with more emotion:

High emotion communication

- Readily talk about their emotions
- Animated facial expressions
- Give strong clues to their internal emotions
- Use a more informal style
- Proactive in encouraging physical contact
- Regularly take conversations off-topic
- Highlight key ideas
- Follow conversations into new topics

Once again, this is learning which it is useful to apply broadly within life, not simply within the arena of developing your career. Use this communications styles learning to notice the different preferences within your family and friends. To help strengthen relationships, remember to sprinkle some of the other person's preferences into the conversation. They will respond to it, but not necessarily know why.

Manager's Note: Learn more about understanding different communication styles and how they can help a manager on page 178 in Part II.

Building rapport using awareness of the personal and strategic sides to life

When you're building rapport with someone, first notice 'how' they communicate. Pay attention to their ask, tell and emotion communication preferences.

Second, listen for 'what' they prefer to talk about. We all have a preference for talking about either more of the 'personal' or more of the 'strategic' sides of our life. The personal side covers relationships, family, leadership, motivation and commitment. The strategic side covers what is often called the business side of things: facts, figures, data, measurement, strategy, progress and goal achievement.

If the person you're talking to has a strong preference for one of these then you can strengthen your level of rapport with them by emphasising their preference in your conversation. Just so you know, if you focus on the side they do not have a preference for, they may find this difficult, uncomfortable or even challenging.

Building rapport using shared interests

You can also build rapport with someone by talking about something you have in common. Play detective and look out for clues which will help. LinkedIn profiles are a rich source online. In a work-place you'll find clues in photographs, posters, calendars and book titles. Even the branded names appearing on pens and bags can help you make a connection by noticing what someone enjoys or cares about. If you've genuine shared interests, then referring to them can help to build understanding and rapport.

It is important these are genuine and not over stated. If the person you are going to talk to has a reputation as an international ocean racer and you've only once been on a boat, a rowing boat, at your local boating lake, then don't claim a common passion for hands-on sailing! Keep to genuine common ground so you don't risk damaging rapport by being discovered stretching the truth.

11

Gap: I need to ask better questions

In every-day life, as well as when we are preparing for a change of role, there are lots of occasions when it is important to ask good questions. You may have been told you need to ask better questions, or be more challenging or perhaps you want to ask searching questions in a positive and creative way. This next section will give you practical ways to improve your questioning and get the outcomes you want.

Open and Closed Questions

There are two basic types of question. closed questions, which can be answered by a simple yes or no and, alternatively, open questions which draw out a longer answer. Use closed questions to confirm facts and opinions or to encourage a choice from a set of options. When you use closed questions you are holding the balance of power in the conversation. Use open questions to draw out information and to engage someone in a more open conversation. Open questions share the balance of power in the conversation.

So, if a closed question is one which can be answered with a yes or no, then what is an open question? Simply put, an open question is one which starts with the following words:

Who? What? When? Where? How? Why?

Be careful using 'Why?'.
The word can make people feel as though they have been put on the spot, or that you are being critical or judgemental. Substitute 'What's the reason' instead of 'why' and you'll hear fewer defensive answers. Instead you'll have a more generative and creative impact.

Using closed questions

Use closed questions when you will benefit from the following characteristics:

- They can be answered with 'yes' or 'no' – so the answer is more 'black and white'
- The answer is easy to understand and is brief
- The person asking the closed questions keeps control of the conversation

This makes closed questions useful in the following situations:

Situation	Example Question
Seeking straightforward information	"Do I need to complete your full application form?" "Is marketing your favourite part of the role?"
Confirming information	"The interview is on Wednesday, isn't it?" "I assume you need someone with statistics experience, am I correct?"

While closed questions can be useful, they are limited by our understanding of the situation or our model of the world. Because we don't know what exactly is going on in someone's head, we can only ask closed questions based on our knowledge of what we think is important. You may have noticed some television interviewers use closed questions as a technique to control the direction of a discussion. It can lead to the interviewee becoming increasingly frustrated as they can't talk about what they feel is important.

Open questions are much more powerful if you wish the other person to feel engaged and involved in the conversation.

Using open questions

Open questions are powerful because they have the following characteristics:

- The person answering needs to give you more information and, while doing so, they may learn something themselves
- The longer answers to an open question can reveal valuable information about emotions and opinions as well as facts
- The answer to an open question can't be predicted so the control of the conversation is given to the person answering the questions

Open questions are highly valuable in the following situations:

Situation	Example Question
Ensuring you have all of the information you need	"What level of vehicle knowledge do you need?" "How many packing lines does this role cover?" "Who are the key stakeholders in this role?"

Gaining a deeper understanding of the other person's point of view	"Which responsibilities do you feel are most important?" "How do you feel about the role?" "What makes this urgent for you?" "What do you enjoy most in your current role?" "What excites you most about this opportunity?"
Understanding the size and shape of an opportunity or issue	"How often does this happen?" "Where else could this occur?" "Who does this matter to?" "What needs to be done first?"
Building rapport with the other person	"How are you today?" "What are you planning to do this weekend?" "How did you enjoy your holiday?"

By waiting for the answer to your open question you hand control of the conversation over to the person you are talking to. You may find they take the conversation in a direction you would never have expected, and provide you with crucial information which would have remained undiscovered had you used a closed question.

Make sure you give the person you're questioning enough time to respond. This may need to include thinking time before they answer, so, rather than interpreting a pause as a 'no comment' and continuing, hold the silence and let them have time to think before moving on. Immediate responses tend to be surface thoughts. By holding an interested silence, you allow them to get deeper into their thinking and draw out more valuable answers.

Remember skilful questioning needs to be matched by careful listening so you understand what someone really means by their answers.

Your body language and tone of voice can also play a part in the answers you receive when you ask questions. If you give the impression you are disinterested or bored, you will get superficial answers so, use your active listening skills to the full.

"The art and science of asking questions
is the source of all knowledge."
Thomas Berger

12

Gap: I need to improve finding out facts and details

Sometimes you'll notice the person you are talking to is using a lot of generalisations and vague statements. It is easy to simply accept these and move on, but often we need to learn more about what is going on by digging out more facts and details.

In this situation use the precision question approach. The first step is to identify the clues to vagueness, and then ask a matching question which pulls out more information. Next you will find a list of these clues and the corresponding questions to improve the level of precision.

You can apply the same approach to yourself. When you ask questions, or want to give a clear message, you will significantly increase your impact if your questions and statements have a good level of precision in them. So, check for the clues to vagueness in what you plan to say, and ask yourself the questions which will draw out that precision.

The clues to poor precision fall into several categories. Key categories are: generalisations, rules, unclear-pronouns and comparators. Here's how to spot the clues and what to do when you notice them.

> **Generalisations**. Describing something in general terms can save us time, but that saving usually reduces our precision, and can leave others guessing or making incorrect assumptions.
>
> Common generalisation words to listen out for and avoid are:
>
> - **All**: For example: "I need help to ensure I know about **all** the advertised vacancies." This request could result in a deluge of emails about every job vacancy, regardless of the suitability of skills requirements, location and salary. Adding a little precision, such as "I need help to ensure I know about the vacancies within 50 miles of here needing strong organisational and written communications skills" will radically increase your chances of receiving what you need.

- **Always**: "I'm **always** being told I'm ready for the next step." Again, it is unlikely that 'always' is accurate, so generalising in this way reduces the impact of the sentence. Adding precision in the form of facts will considerably boost the influence of what you say. For example: "I've been told twice, by our HR director, I am ready for the next step up."

- **Everyone**: "I want to get feedback from **everyone** to help my application." This generalisation could make obtaining feedback feel like an onerous task. Adding some precision can make a task feel much more achievable, for example: "I want to get feedback from two members of our team plus yourself and two of my customers."

- **Never**: "I'll **never** have the right experience to match what the recruiters want." This generalisation can easily become self-limiting because it's creating an immovable block. The more we use self-limiting phrases, the more we start to believe them. Changing this generalisation to: "I don't yet have the level of basic report-writing skills and presentation experience the recruiters want" builds in precision and replaces the immovable block with specific goals which are achievable and motivating and give a strong clue as to how someone could help you.

Rules: Introducing a 'rule' word into what we say can discourage us from exploring and explaining what we mean clearly because the word implies some form of bad consequence will occur for not obeying the rule.

Common 'rule' words to listen out for and avoid are:

- **Should**: "I feel I **should** apply for this job because I have ...." In this example, 'should' suggests some inevitability, or a lack of personal choice, which is not the impression we want to give when asking for help. Simply changing 'should' to 'can' places control back with ourselves: "I can apply for this role because I have…"

- **Must**: "I **must** be patient and just wait to see what comes along." Using 'must' can create a block to alternatives which may be more beneficial to us. We can communicate more meaning by replacing 'must' with a little more information: "I can either wait to see what comes along or I can set a deadline for how long I'll wait, or I can start taking action now."

- **Shouldn't**: "They **shouldn't** need more information about what I want." Here, using 'shouldn't' prevents us from exploring more precision and alternatives and, while it may be true, there is a risk we are wrong. Using "I've given them what I feel is sufficient information but I will check they have what they need" will drive out more precision and understanding.

- **Can't**: "I **can't** do the budgeting part of the job." Using this 'rule' word helps us avoid the task of being precise about what it would take to be successful. Some fact-finding can support us understanding with more precision what we do need, which opens up new possibilities. For example: "I will be able to the budgeting part of the job if I get some basic understanding of how spreadsheets work."

Unclear pronouns: Using unclear pronouns can again speed up our communications, but at the risk of leaving the meaning too vague. So vague that those we talk to are left confused, or have to work hard to understand us. They simply make an instant assumption, rightly or wrongly, about who or what we mean.

Common unclear pronouns to listen out for and avoid are:

- **They**: "When I go for an interview I need to make sure **they** have my CV."

- **She and He**: My advisor told me **he** was the person to check my application.

Often, we believe the context is very clear when we use 'they', 'he' and 'she'. In our own heads the context may indeed be very solid. However, what's in our own head and what's in someone else's head can be very different, so add the precision of using names or titles. As well as synchronising your understanding with others, you have opened up the possibility of receiving a helpful suggestion about someone you may have forgotten.

Comparators: Comparator words give a general sense of our meaning by appearing to relate what we describe to something else. But the 'something else' is usually missing and our words will lack the precision to communicate a good understanding which means the person we are communicating with again has to work harder before they can contribute.

Common comparator words to listen out for and avoid are:

- **Too much**: "I don't want **too much** travel in the job." This example lacks precision about the amount of travel which will be acceptable. It could encourage the listener to assume that their own interpretation of 'too much travel' is the same as yours, unless they're prepared to invest valuable time asking you what you really mean. A change to: "I want a job in which I will travel for up to three days each month, to keep my work-life balance." gives specific information which can be acted upon or negotiated.

- **Too many**: "There will be **too many** ideas to mention." Using 'too many' is a short-cut which removes precision. There are no facts here about how many ideas are over the acceptable limit and the words introduce a block to finding a way forward. Switching to "I have five ideas to talk about, but there's only time for three" immediately starts to catalyse new thinking about solutions.

- **Best**: "If I get this job, I will do my **best** for you." This is a pleasant sentiment to hear, but how do we know what their 'best' is, and whether it matches what the job demands? Be specific about what 'best' means. For example: "If I get this job, I'll meet each of your targets and I'll also help your team build relationships with new clients."

- **Worst**: "That was the **worst** idea." Rather than avoid specifics by using 'worst', simply add a fact or two which conveys what is important to you. For example: "That idea didn't work because the technology is still unreliable and our clients changed what they needed."

Quality: A special example of a word which we hear used frequently, and which evokes a wide variation in understanding is 'quality'.

If you ask for a 'quality car' then your request might be interpreted in a number of ways. Is it the type of car which has rapid acceleration to a high speed or one which has zero emissions? Is it one which can pull a heavy load over rough terrain or one which will fit into the smallest city parking place? Unless you provide more precision, you have no idea of how 'quality' has been interpreted and, as in this example, the results of your request could be very unexpected. Tune in to how many times you hear 'a quality product', 'world class quality', 'highest quality', or 'poor quality' and let each one remind you to be more specific about what you really mean.

Using precision questions, you will not only improve your own understanding but will potentially also improve the understanding of the person you are talking to.

Neil learned this while talking to a senior scout leader who needed help in recruiting new scout leaders. Their conversation sounded like this:

> Senior Scout Leader: "I need to recruit new scout leaders and can't find enough candidates with the right experience."
>
> Neil: "So what experience do they need?"
>
> Senior Scout Leader: "Well my existing scout leaders have experience of being section leaders."
>
> Neil: "<u>All</u> of them?"
>
> Senior Scout Leader: "Well not <u>all</u> of them, I've one or two who weren't section leaders but they've been really good too."
>
> Neil: "So if you widen your search to include people who've not been section leaders what does that mean?"
>
> Senior Scout Leader: "All of a sudden I can think of 10 more possible candidates!"

Asking precision questions gives you the opportunity to persist in a conversation more than you might have done before.
Imagine a future conversation with a recruiting manager during which she says "All of my current staff have experience in marketing."

If you haven't had experience in the marketing field, you can either quit at that point or persist by gently probing at the use of the word 'experience' which is a commonly used, but vague word.

You can learn more by asking "Just so I understand, what level of experience do they all have in marketing?"

One reply may be "All of them have a masters in marketing. It's so vital for this role" but another may be "Now you ask, there is quite a variety in the levels. Some have been on a one-day awareness course we run internally, others have academic marketing qualifications, and the rest have worked in a marketing department for a year or more."

So your question will help you to uncover more and understand more.

You could also challenge the first response by asking about what makes marketing experience vital or asking what other experience would be useful to their organisation.

Whichever approach you take, your precision questions will take you a bit deeper than just accepting a superficial answer, and you are demonstrating your commitment to understanding fully.

"Assumptions are dangerous things to make,
and like all dangerous things to make -- bombs,
for instance, or strawberry shortcake -- if you make even the
tiniest mistake you can find yourself in terrible trouble."
Lemony Snicket

13

Gap: I need to ask searching questions while maintaining good relationships

Have you ever had an occasion when you have asked a question and got a surprisingly negative or defensive response?

It's a common situation and, when we reflect for a moment, perhaps we can identify that we had some part in creating it because we didn't set the context of the question correctly, and its meaning was misinterpreted, or an unhelpful motive was assumed by the listener.

You can significantly improve your chances of receiving a constructive response to your questions if the person you are talking to understands what's on your mind, and what your intent is, when you ask the question. The question can be challenging, but because they understand more about the reason for asking it, they can answer without interfering with the relationship you have developed.

'Signalling' and your choice of question are important to achieve this.

When choosing the *type* of question, first think about what you want to achieve.

Is it to get to a precise fact or is it a longer response where an open question would come in useful? Remember to avoid the word "Why?" as that can come across as directly challenging. "For what reason?", or "What's the reason?" are gentler-sounding alternatives.

Second, plan a little signalling before you ask your question. Signalling can be as simple as adding a couple of words to the front of your question so the other person understands your intent. Signalling reduces the risk that they'll assume the question is meant to be deliberately unhelpful to them.

Here are examples, shown in italics, of useful signalling phrases to place in front of your questions:

"Just so I understand more fully, how does that help?"
"I'm curious. Who works at the ….?"
"To help me be absolutely clear on this, how often ….?"
"So we both benefit from the work finishing on time, how soon could ...?"
While I know there are no current vacancies, I'm interested to find out …."

By adding this type of phrase at the beginning of your questions you'll give the other person some idea of your intent, and even give them some clues as to what kind of answer you are looking for.

14

Gap: I need to boost my self confidence and self-talk

Many of us are advised to 'be more confident' in work and beyond but rarely does that advice come with a 'how to do it' guide. In this section is a technique which we and our clients have found consistently works well. It's simple and just needs a little concentration to make it work for you.

To boost your self-confidence, first appreciate that the way you speak to yourself directly affects your confidence level. 'Self-talk' directs your thought patterns and directly influences how you feel about yourself. Some self-talk is positive and helpful while some can be very negative and seriously undermine your self-esteem.

Fortunately, you can take action. By changing the way you talk to yourself, you can improve your confidence, so you feel better and others benefit more from what you do.

Most of what we read and watch about people 'talking to themselves' describes it in a negative way. The reality, however, is most of us do talk to ourselves. Often it is through our inner voice, silently inside our heads. Sometimes it is audible.

When we listen to our self-talk we give it a lot of influence. That internal chatter can be the equivalent of a cheer-leader, boosting your confidence and encouraging new ideas, or it can be a nagging commentator, always finding fault, criticising, undermining your success.

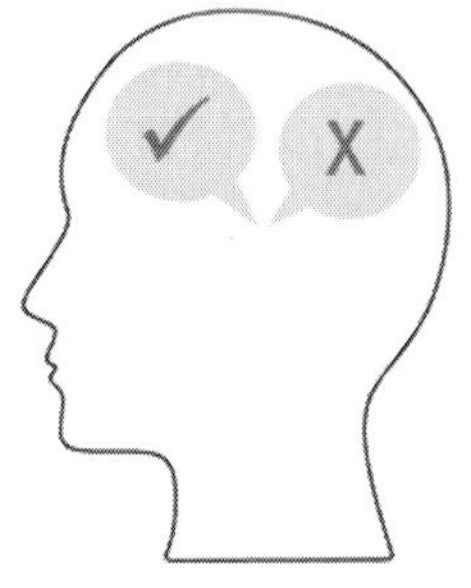

So, that's why you're reading about self-talk here. As you take action to fill the gaps, between what you have now and what you need for your next role, some of that internal chatter is going to occur. It's your choice whether the chatter is helpful to you or not.

In many sports, we hear of sportswomen and sportsmen 'getting their head into the game'. We see them talking out loud to themselves to encourage higher levels of performance. It's interesting to listen to what they choose to say, and what the effect is. If they choose to use the "come on, you can do better than this" or "that's good, do it again" type of positive affirmation, they tend to pick up or sustain their own performance. If they start to talk themselves down, then their performance drops off very rapidly. The great players carefully choose how they react to the game around them and target their internal conversation and thoughts so the outcome is positive and strengthening.

Put simply, our actions are inspired by our thoughts, so when you change the way you think and change what you say to yourself, you make a change to the actions you take. By using more positive self-talk you can positively influence your performance.

Use this technique for your own benefit. It's free!

Control Your Self-Talk

Take a moment now to remember the last time something worked well for you. Choose a memorable occasion.

What did you say to yourself or think to yourself at that time? A positive self-talk example of what you might have said is:

"Good result! Asking for help and concentrating on accuracy really worked. Next time I'll also add more ideas and make it look even better."

That positive self-talk was a short self-congratulation on the success; a reflection on the important things which led to that success, and a note of an improvement to make to achieve an even better result next time.

Negative self-talk, even when something went well, may sound like:

"It was ok, but I made so many mistakes and that's disappointing, I shouldn't make mistakes," or "I should have done even better" or "It must have been simple if I managed it."

Now, think back to the last time something didn't go well for you. What did you say to yourself, or think to yourself, then?

Negative self-talk, for an activity that went badly, may have sounded like "I can't do this," or "It's too difficult," or "I shouldn't have tried," or "It happens every time," or "What is wrong with me? If only I had...."

Use positive self-talk, even though something went badly. An example of this is:

"Well that didn't go as well as I wanted, but three out of four stages did finish on time, nobody's perfect, and I now know in future I need to involve the engineers earlier to get the right result."

Make your self-talk work for you

Self-talk is very powerful so make your self-talk work positively for you. Take these steps to put your negative self-talk into the past and switch to positive, helpful self-talk.

- **Become aware of your self-talk**. Once you're aware of it you can move on to making improvements to it.
- **Be specific, don't generalise.** If you do find your self-talk is negative, rephrase any generalisations so they're more specific. For example, "My meetings go off topic" changes to "Today's item about pensions went off topic, but the rest went well."
- **Refer to negative incidents in the past tense.** When you self-talk in the present tense about negative things: "My timekeeping is terrible" it reinforces a continuous negative perception. Instead, refer to negative things in the past tense: "My time keeping for the pensions meeting was out by two minutes." This allows for the possibility your timekeeping will improve in the future and you have some power of choice over this.

- **Challenge negative rules.** When you hear yourself saying "I shouldn't do that" challenge yourself by asking yourself "What would happen if you did?" and then turn your self-talk from "I shouldn't do that" to "I can do this, and this."

- **When you use your self-talk to challenge yourself use 'you' instead of 'I' or 'me'.** For example, ask yourself: "What would happen if you did challenge the result?" Saying 'you' creates a psychological distance between yourself and the situation, which makes it more comfortable and interesting to think about.

- **Choose positive affirmation** – flip the coin. Just as a coin has two faces, many situations have more than one way to look at them. Choose to emphasise the positive and creative elements in your self-talk, as well as being specific and realistic about the negative elements. You can use this powerfully in your general conversations too. Instead of "We're stalled, waiting for John to sign the contract" say "Let's decide what to get done while we're waiting for John to sign."

- **Avoid using 'try'.** Try is a word you may have used in your self-talk and in your general conversations. It's a word which sounds positive but when you examine it a bit more closely it is used to create or allow the possibility of failure. For example, if you compare "I'll try and make time to write a chapter of the book today" with the alternative "I will make time to write a chapter of the book today", which one of those statements is more positive and deterministic?

  Without realising it, we may have been using the word try so we have an excuse readily available in case it doesn't happen. An excuse like "Well, I only said I'd try and other things got in the way."

  Notice when you are about to use the word try and simply

remove the word. Instead, be definite about what you *will* do. If it doesn't work out, that's fine. Learn from what caused it to not happen.

When we use try in our conversations we risk setting an unrealistic expectation which will be unhelpful later.

If you hear "I'll try to get the information on your desk by the end of Wednesday," you'll probably remember hearing 'Wednesday' and your mental plans will be designed around having their information by the end of that day.

But what if they meant there's only a small possibility of delivering the information by the end of Wednesday and it's much more likely it will arrive on Friday?

You would benefit more from hearing "I'll push for delivering it by the end of Wednesday, but it will definitely be with you by the end of Friday.' Now you have clarity for your planning.

Be clear in what you say, so others know what you are committing to. When you notice someone say try in a conversation with you, just ask a question so that you know precisely what they mean. For example, if you hear "I'll try to get there by 9 o'clock" you can ask "When can you guarantee you'll be there?" The answer you get may be a confirmation "Oh, I mean I *will* be there by 9 o'clock" or the answer may flush out important information, "Well, I need to get some petrol on the way so let's say we'll meet at 9.15."

- Use self-talk as though you are talking to a friend. We've all overheard somebody say words about us which aren't helpful. That's life and we can decide how we deal with it. But why would we talk to ourselves in this way? You have the choice, so talk to yourself as if you were talking to a good friend: with respect and compassion and with an objective not to destroy, only create.

Reflect on these quotations as you prepare to move on.

" *The more man meditates upon good thoughts, the better will be his world and the world at large.*"
Confucius

"*No one can make you feel inferior without your consent.*"
Eleanor Roosevelt

"*Your opinion of yourself becomes your reality.*"
50 Cent

15

Gap: I need to change my attitude

We worked in an office with a rather curious sign hanging above the entrance. It had the following invitation.

CHOOSE YOUR ATTITUDE

Do you consistently choose your attitude, or do you allow your attitude to be set by external circumstances? An example of the latter is a person who spends their day in a foul mood because they were delayed by heavy traffic on the way to work. Or the person who has had an argument with a family member over breakfast, and is grumpy with their colleagues all morning. You may even hear the excuse "I've just had something bad happen, so forgive me for being in a bad temper."

Some circumstances are good and some less so, but we always have a personal choice of which attitude we adopt. We can't control events, but we can control how we respond to them.

The ability to choose the attitude we hold is something which can benefit us in many circumstances. It's especially important when we're planning our own personal development.

Take a moment to choose your attitude each day.

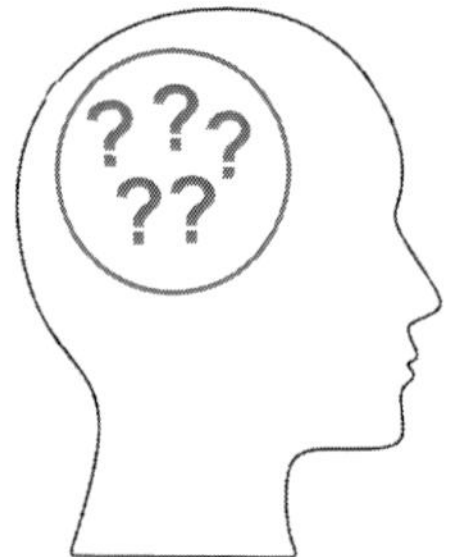

What attitude will you take towards your personal development?

Which attitude will serve you best in your workplace?

"Whether your life is happy or not
is your own choice.
Many people think I can't live a normal life
because I don't have arms or legs.
I could choose to believe that.
I choose to be happy."
Nick Vujicic

16

Gap: I need to be more adaptable

Job role descriptions often describe adaptability as a desired or essential attribute. It may be a behaviour which is natural to you already and if not, be confident it's a behaviour you can learn.

There are different levels of adaptability, and one of your tasks is to decide which level suits you, and which level is needed in the role you're preparing for.

Adaptability can be described as the way you behave when change is needed. Someone with an interest in adaptability will respond creatively when changes are asked for. Alternatively, they may be the person who catalyses change. They'll search out ways to make a change work, and may make suggestions for improvements which will help a change become more effective.

They often find motivation from the challenge of making changes work.

Those with less interest in adaptability will tend to find more reasons not to change from the status quo, and will be motivated by keeping things consistent, well ordered and well established.

The extremes of adaptability have their challenges. Someone who continually adapts and changes daily or hourly can be very hard to work with in a team, since it takes some effort for the rest of the team to catch up with the latest situation. In extreme cases this continuous adapting can get in the way of delivering an outcome because there is too much change going on.

At the other extreme, someone who never adapts can hold back change causing processes to stagnate and become out of date. Again, this extreme can affect team working because the team feel they are being slowed down by the lack of change.

It's a harsh reality that there's rarely any specific measure to describe how much adaptability should be happening. Imagine working in a fast-evolving mobile-phone development company. A high frequency of adaptability is essential in the research and development organisation who are designing software to meet fast-changing consumer needs and trends. But, in that same mobile phone company, the manufacturing organisation will have a much lower frequency for adaptability because, once a phone starts to roll off the manufacturing line, consistency in the quality of manufacture is essential. Only when a new phone hits the production process must the adaptability re-emerge, to change the line so it can successfully and consistently produce the next batch of phones.

To improve your adaptability, first be clear about the purpose behind what you are doing, and regularly check to see if it's changed.

Adaptability is the behaviour we use to find new ways to achieve the purpose we are aiming for. For instance, if there's a fuel strike we can adapt by getting to work on a bike and achieve our purpose of getting to work, earning money and moving towards living the life we want.

If an organisation releases employees, it's adapting so it can continue to meet its purpose: remaining competitive, earning income, supporting its investors and customers.

When there is a new baby in the family we may need to adapt by moving to a new house to meet the purpose of providing a comfortable home for the family.

Sometimes the purpose changes: A national rail network terminates rail lines because its purpose has changed from providing transport for all to making money for its investors.

Make sure you know the purpose behind the activities you deliver.

If the purpose changes, be prepared to start identifying what related changes you'll need to make so you can achieve the new purpose.

When the purpose remains consistent, keep an eye out for changes which mean you could achieve the purpose faster, cheaper or with improved quality.

When someone proposes changes to you, talk to them about the purpose which drives your work. This may be a business deliverable or it may be a personal driver. You'll then find it easier to discuss how a proposed change will impact on you achieving your purpose.

You can be adaptable by being positive and encouraging, and willing to cooperate with those changes which will complement your achievement. You can also encourage alternative solutions to be developed if any proposed changes will have a negative impact on your achievement.

17

Gap: I need to improve my decision-making

You're experienced in making decisions every day, so you know you can do it at some level. If you become aware that you need to improve your decision making, here are four short tips which will help.

1. Not all decisions are equal: The impact of some decisions is much more significant than others, so treat them differently. When it's time to make a low impact decision, make it quickly and move on. Review regularly whether a decision still has the same level of impact as before. For example, the first large order with a supplier may need a

detailed decision process to review the supplier and their capabilities. The decision to make follow-up orders could be much quicker; just a brief check to confirm that the product or service remains appropriate, then the decision is made.

2. Promptly start higher impact decision-making: A high impact decision may need more steps and time, but it's important you begin and avoid procrastinating. Make a judgement. Ask yourself "Is there an overwhelming benefit from delaying this decision, or can I get it started now?"

3. Use both logical reasoning and emotion: both of these can contribute to your decision, but make sure you flush out what part each is playing and don't ignore either.

For example, a group of engineers fought back hard when their finance team told them their components supplier was changing. The logical reasoning was solid. The new supplier was cheaper and promised the same quality. The savings would be used to give the sales team new office equipment. But the emotional considerations were missing. The engineers had a strong relationship with the old supplier who would lend them experts to develop new parts and then create all the drawings. This saved the engineers enormous amounts of time and energy. The new supplier didn't offer these services, so the engineers were concerned about having a smaller budget plus a much higher workload they couldn't deliver in time to meet their deadlines.

It's equally important to consider the logical reasoning when the emotional influencers are strong too.

4. Quality, Time, Cost: As you make your decisions, remember the connection between quality, time and cost. If something needs to be made faster, then there's likely to be a change in the quality, the cost or both. If something needs to become cheaper then there's likely to be a change in quality, time or both. If the quality needs to increase, then there's likely to be a change to the cost or time or both.

   Use the time, quality, cost relationship to quickly assess some of the impact a decision may have, so the impact doesn't emerge as a surprise later on.

"The key to good decision making is not knowledge.
It is understanding.
We are swimming in the former.
We are desperately lacking in the latter."
Malcolm Gladwell

18

Gap: I need to become 'more visible'

A colleague of ours returned from his performance review discussion clutching a piece of paper.

He replied to our questioning looks with "Oh, it went quite well but still no opportunities to move to a new role. My boss wrote down what I need to do. But it just says 'Sam needs to be more visible.' What am I supposed to do to improve that?"

On the face of it 'be more visible' sounds straight forward if we have been scurrying around the work-place in stealth mode, hiding in shadows and only walking out in the open during the hours of darkness. But as most of us don't do that, the feedback of 'be more visible' can feel unexpected and puzzling. If you think back to the section on precision questions, you'll recognise this as an example of very poor precision from the person giving feedback. And what do you do when you notice poor precision? Yes, ask questions.

The reason for more visibility

What is the purpose of becoming more visible? In the context of finding your next role, the reason for being asked to be more visible is often because your manager needs to persuade other managers that you should be considered for a role. Managers can be averse to risk, so even if your boss gives you a glowing report, some of their peers will be uncomfortable considering you unless a) they have personally experienced what you do and how you do it, or b) they know someone, who isn't your boss, who has personally experienced what you do and how you do it.

Decide what visibility you need

If you receive the feedback that you need to 'be more visible', here are three questions you need to ask before you take action:

1. **Who needs to see me?** You could spend a lot of time and effort demonstrating what you do and how you do it, only to find the people who have seen you do not have any influence on the decision for your next role. So, find out. Who are the critical individuals you need to be visible to? It may be a specific manager, an HR specialist or someone who isn't a manager but who is an important influencer. If promotion or selection decisions are made by a committee, you may need to identify who has the decision-making authority in the group.

2. **What do they need to see?** You could demonstrate lots of activities in front of the right people, only to find they needed to see you demonstrate something completely different. By asking what they need to see, you'll find out whether it's something you're capable of doing now (and they just haven't seen it) or something you'll need to develop further and demonstrate to them. By asking your manager for support you may be able to get a temporary position in another team, or work on a different project so you can be visible to those who need to see you.

3. **What's going to help convince them?** Are they going to be convinced by seeing you work with very little communication with peers and managers, or will they want to see you as a continual communicator? Will they want to see you sticking to agreed processes, and encouraging others to do the same, or will they want to see you creatively challenging the status quo to encourage new ideas and improvements? Find out the important convincers for these influential stakeholders.

   Remember different people have different approaches to being convinced. Here are the common ones:

Automatic	Is immediately convinced An early adopter
Period of time	Likes trial periods and thinking time
Number of times	Is convinced after seeing repeated good performance
Consistent	Maintains their original opinion May never be truly convinced

When you've decided 'who needs to see me?', 'what do they need to see?', and 'what's going to help convince them?', you'll already be in a much stronger position of knowing what you are aiming for, and ready to make it happen.

Tips to increase your visibility

There are lots of simple ways to build greater visibility for yourself. Here are our tips. Take a moment to decide which tips match the kind of visibility you know you need, and which tips may help you develop the general visibility you'd like to have in the future.

Add your name. Add your name to what you do. Reports, presentations, leaflets, posters, anything which will get your name out there. This contributes to a wider familiarity with who you are and what you do so people say "Yes, I've seen her name on some great work."

Build your network. If someone has met you, they are much more likely to talk about you, recommend you and even trust you. Building good relationships can even be more influential than demonstrating deep skills and experience. Leaders like to know someone will be good to work with, and will fit with their team. Compare that with having someone join the team with 100% of the specialist experience but who continually annoys and disrupts the rest of the team.

You can approach building your network in a very sharply focused way, finding out who needs to be influenced and building connections with them, as well as with those whose opinions they listen to.

Our recommendation is to include that sense of focus (so you are building connections with the influencers you know) but also build your network more widely. Someone unexpected could be in a position to help or hinder your progress.

Piotr shared a story about a surprise in his network:

> "I was building connections with the leaders I felt were most influential to my next role while I continued to maintain my existing network. A coffee conversation with a colleague surprised me when he revealed he was a close friend to one of these leaders, and told me he'd be happy to mention my name and my aspirations next time they went out for a beer."

Remember to find opportunities to help others while you are networking too, so it isn't a one-direction process. "What's on your mind and how could my network help?" is a simple way of offering.

Show interest in meeting others and share what you know. Raise your visibility by asking to meet people outside your usual circle of contacts. This can be to learn more about their roles, or about their part of the organisation. Most people will be pleased to spend a few minutes to talk to someone about what they do. Explain that the reason you're asking is to help you broaden your understanding in readiness for future a role.

Offer to attend the meetings of other groups to explain about your role, team or organisation, or simply to share best practice. You could provide a refreshing change to their agenda and the worst that can happen is they say no thanks.

Volunteer. Volunteer to join another team or a working party. Take on extra responsibilities which fit with your direction: the experience you want to develop, the skills you want to demonstrate, or the connections you want to make.

Record what you have accomplished. Keep a list of your accomplishments and add to it as you achieve more. If you aren't keeping track of your accomplishments, who do you think is? Remember to celebrate them in whatever way works for you, and if you find a period of time when no accomplishments occur to you, think more deeply and listen to what others say. If there is nothing new emerging, then use that as a signal to take action. How can you turn something you are doing into an accomplishment? What else could you do?

Ask for feedback. Ask for feedback in a structured planned-ahead way. Decide what feedback you want to hear at a certain time. Decide what you'll need to do so you'll be comfortable asking for the feedback and the person will be in a good position to provide the feedback you want. The step of thinking about feedback for you helps them form opinions about you, which may not have been conscious before. They are then much more likely to share their opinions with others.

Make time for talk. If you normally get to work and concentrate solely on doing your job, you're missing out on the potential of relationships which develop when you talk more socially with people. Your future is worth investing in, so schedule a little time each day or each week to loiter a little in communal spaces, like around the coffee machine. Talk to people, demonstrate being human! Remember, now you are being more visible you have the opportunity to help set the tone or culture of the place you want to work in.

Practise keeping your conversations positive. Don't verbally encourage conversations to spiral down into criticism of other people, how poorly other teams work, or how lacking the leadership is. If you want to contribute to these conversations, simply flip the tone and talk about what you do want to hear. Become known as someone who searches for solutions, not someone who dwells endlessly on what's wrong.

Share praise. Give praise to others for good work and deliver it in front of peers and managers. Talk about issues and problems more privately. Be generous in giving credit where it's due. This doesn't draw attention away from you, instead it demonstrates a leadership quality respected by many.

Chose mentors carefully. Mentors can give you good advice which you can use to your benefit. Juice up the benefits by asking for mentoring from someone to whom you need to be 'more visible.' Not only do you become more visible to them physically, you can share what your goals are, highlight your strengths and where you need to develop, and ask for their help. You also get the opportunity to pick up clues about what's important to them. Useful information for when you need to convince them to support you for a new role.

Share your opinion and your disagreements. Quietly nodding and agreeing doesn't attract attention. If you know about a subject, and don't agree, make it clear what your opinion is. Be prepared to be persuaded otherwise, but recognise your opinion can catalyse better thinking and decisions. Ask open ended questions which drill down to get detail, or zoom-out to get the bigger picture and purpose.

Prepare for the meetings you are invited to and make them work for you. You can boost the value of attending simply by reading the agenda and spending one minute to note three desired outcomes you have from the meeting. The desired outcomes may relate directly to the agenda items and your contribution, or they may relate you something you want personally out of the meeting to contribute towards your next role.

For example, the following are desired outcomes you could set for when you attend a meeting to agree interview-questions. Desired outcomes are best written in the past tense:

> **Desired outcome 1**: I proposed two interview questions and the meeting agreed their use during interviews.
>
> **Desired outcome 2**: The leaders at the meeting recognise I can contribute to subjects outside my own specialism.
>
> **Desired outcome 3**: The leaders at the meeting heard me praising others for their ideas and contributions, demonstrating I give credit to those who earned it.

Do your existing role well. As you prepare for your next role, the foundation you are working from is your existing role. Plan your 'visibility' activities so they fit around, and integrate with, successfully accomplishing your day to day activities.

This is self-promotion – keep it positive. Becoming 'more visible' is about self-promotion. That's ok. If you aren't taking steps to communicate your value, and draw attention to your value, then those influential leaders could remain unaware of the benefits you could bring them. Remember to keep your self-promotion positive and creative. Keep conversations moving forward, even if you have disagreements. Make it clear you are willing to be persuaded differently, so you become known, not for arrogance, but for being constructive.

Look around you and start to notice who else uses these 'visibility' techniques. When you notice something that works, copy it and use it yourself. You can now decide on your plan for increasing your visibility. Remember to ask others for their help in achieving it.

19

Gap: I need to prepare for talking to recruiting managers

A question we are often asked when career coaching is "What do recruiting managers want to know and how do I prepare?" The answer can be determined at a number of different levels.

Before answering the question though, a short warning. Prepare for the 'informal chat.'

The informal chat

The 'informal chat' regularly occurs when the recruiting manager is within the same company as yourself, but can also occur when a recruiting manager is hiring outside their company. The message you receive is they would like you to pop in for a chat about potential opportunities, nothing formal.

Remember: Before you answer their invitation, be assured you must prepare for this 'casual chat' like you would an interview.

Ellie, a friend of ours, shared with us her story of how she was caught out by a 'casual chat'.

"I had applied for three jobs and was invited to interview for two of them. I prepared well and the interviews felt very productive and positive. While I was waiting for the hiring decisions to be announced I received an email about the third job. The email was from Julie who said she liked what she read in my CV and would enjoy meeting up over a coffee for a casual chat to tell me more about the job. I agreed and met Julie outside the office where she worked. But instead of heading for a coffee shop she told me there were a couple more people who would like to join in the conversation and opened the door into a large boardroom. The black table had an empty chair on one side and five chairs along the other. All of which were now occupied with suits! Oh no! And I didn't even get a coffee!"

Perhaps you won't find a boardroom behind the door when you arrive for your informal chat, but remember their agenda will be to find out more about you and what you know, as well as to tell you about their opportunities.

If you are the person initiating the informal chat, for example to learn more about an organisation you'd like to work in, remember to prepare for the discussion by being clear about what role you'd like to do and what skills you bring with you. We have clients, colleagues and our own experiences of these informal conversations moving rapidly into detailed discussions about developing a missing role in the organisation and leading to a job offer.

This happens because your conversations and interest can catalyse new ideas for the person you're meeting. That increases the chance they discover there's a job which needs to be done and realise your enthusiasm and skills will help.

Preparing to talk to a recruiting manager

Regardless of whether a recruiting manager is in your existing organisation or a different organisation, they are going to want to understand more about you before they consider you for a role. A quick search online will reveal lots of information to help you prepare for these conversations, so here we will simply offer you a common sense starting point.

- **Do some research before talking to a recruiting manager**. Know what the job really is, not just the job title. Recruiting managers are busy people. You can earn some recognition by describing what you know and asking them to help add more information. If you were the recruiting manager, compare how you'd feel if one candidate started the conversation with "Tell me, what is this job?" and the next candidate started with "I've been able to find out this job involves ...." One sounds proactive and interested, the other a lot less so.

- **Describe the skills, knowledge and experience, involved in the job which you already possess.**
  Research the job and first describe the job requirements you have now which will enable you to do the job essentials. Then describe those you will need to develop further while doing the job.
  Recruiting managers want to be convinced you're right for the job, so prepare what you'll say beforehand, then explain this clearly during the conversation. Even if they don't ask you directly, make sure you still tell them.

- **Describe how you will fit into their organisation.** Employers need to know you are going to fit with their existing organisation, ways of working and culture. This could either mean you're a perfect match for their team, or you'll bring some important difference to their team and work. Research what you can to find out about the culture, how the organisation operates and its values. Describe how you have worked in their preferred way in the past. Ask questions to find out what else is important about the way the job must be done. This will give you the opportunity to decide for yourself how well you match the job and the organisation as well as giving you the opportunity to describe more about your experience and how it supports you being the right person for the job.

- **Tell them you are interested in the job, and want the job!**
  Employers want to know you have a real interest in their job and you want it! Perhaps you are assuming 'Well, I've applied so they must know I am interested'. But unless you say out loud "I'm interested in this job and I do want this job" the recruiter will simply not be certain and alternative candidates, who are more enthusiastic, may steal their attention.

Taking these steps will demand a little research ahead of the interview. Plan ahead so you can make enquiries through your network, or telephone the recruiting manager, or ask to speak to someone doing the job now. Even if this preparation only adds an extra 20% to the positive impression you give, don't you want a 20% advantage?

Invest time researching the role you want. Do your research for each role you express interest in.

Think about what you'd do to develop the role further, and how you might drive improvements. Understand what some of the challenges are in the role and where you'll need to personally develop. Have a range of questions prepared which you can discuss with the recruiting manager. Questions which demonstrate you've not just looked at the job advertisement, but have also done the research and thinking that demonstrate your real interest.

20

Gap: I need to show more persistence

Calvin Coolidge once said:

"Nothing in the world can take the place of persistence. Talent will not; nothing is more common than unsuccessful men with talent."

We live in a world where the press fuel an impression that many of the successful people we know have benefited from instant success. The reality is the vast majority of these people have worked hard, failed, worked hard again, failed and so on until they eventually found their success. For example:

> NASA experienced 20 failures in its first 28 attempts to send rockets into space.

> James Dyson made 5127 prototypes before he perfected his bagless vacuum cleaner. He almost went bankrupt on several occasions and all of the leading manufactures of vacuum cleaners refused to make the product, driving him to set up his own manufacturing company and eventually become the world's first billionaire inventor.

The reason they succeed is because, yes, they have some level of talent, but also because they have a high level of persistence.

Psychological research literature has convincingly described the relationship between talent and persistence, in its simplest form, as:

Performance = Ability x Persistence

(Campbell, J. P. et al 1993)

So, if someone has a great ability but no persistence, then performance will be lost. Similarly, high persistence but zero ability will kill performance too. A mix of some talent and a strong level of persistence can work wonders.

As you take your steps to fill the gaps to bring you closer to your next role, remind yourself that you know the performance you need can come from developing a modest level of talent, propelled by a plentiful helping of persistence.

JK Rowling was a single mother who was struggling financially when she wrote the first Harry Potter book. Twelve publishers rejected the manuscript. The publisher who finally said yes also advised her to get a paying job because writing children's books wouldn't make her any money. She's now one of the richest women in the world because she had some talent, and lots and lots of persistence.

When she talked about those early times, Rowling told an audience at Harvard, "You might never fail on the scale I did but it is impossible to live without failing at something, unless you live so cautiously you might as well not have lived at all, in which case, you fail by default."

Take inspiration from her words and be willing to step a little beyond your comfort zone to fill those gaps.

Be keen to apply your persistence to finding your next role, and use positive self-talk to strengthen your persistence to the level you need to achieve what you want.

21

Take action!

Now you're able to describe the role you want, with its characteristic skills, knowledge, experience and behaviours. You've also developed a solid picture of your strengths, and the gaps you need to work on, so you're in the perfect position to start making progress towards your goal.

Knowing what you're aiming for and where you're starting from may be all you need to get going. If that's you then go! If a little more structure will help you get from 'a' to 'b' then creating a plan will work well for you.

The power of a having a plan: for you and for others

Having a plan will:

- Help you describe to others what you are doing, the reasons, and how they can help.
- Help you divide what you need to do into manageable stages, so any challenges feel achievable and motivating.
- Help you focus your time and effort into delivering the few outcomes which will have the most impact on achieving your goal. It gives you a stronger sense of control over your career and life.
- Help you notice your progress so you can celebrate your achievements as you accomplish them. Equally a plan helps you notice a lack of progress, reminding you to set careful priorities and reach out for help and support.

Having a plan focused on your goal reminds you to regularly review how you describe your goal. This gives you the opportunity to make adjustments and decide if your adjusted goal demands any changes to your plan.

The structure of your plan

Your plan needs to have a structure which matches how you work and how you will use it. If you enjoy working at a summary-level, then create your plan at a summary level. If you enjoy working at summary level but know in your heart you really need to add more precision to make your plan truly effective, then add more precision. Describe the stages in your plan as outcomes, rather than tasks. You can find a reminder of how to create powerful outcomes in the section Have a towards approach on page 77.

If you like to work at a more detailed level, then add just enough detail to meet your needs. Check the level of detail you are using maintains your feeling of motivation. If the detail starts to become unhelpful for you, then concentrate on describing precise outcomes and reduce the number of tasks.

The template shown in the appendix Your Personal Change Planning Template on page 298 will make a good starting point for your plan. It prompts you to describe your goal, the role you want, and also your starting point, your strengths and gaps.

It then prompts you to describe the steps to get from your starting point to your goal, and it encourages you to think about what you want to leave behind as well as what you'd like to keep and develop as you move to your new role.

Adjust the template to suit your needs. Add dates so you have a timeline to work to. Add the names of people who can help you, and how they can help.

Make the plan on your own and then share it with others. Give them the opportunity to ask questions which will prompt your thinking. There are some example questions on the pages following the template. You can ask yourself the same questions, which will help in developing your thinking and your plan. But do ask someone else to ask you the same questions too. Our minds operate differently when a question comes from outside our own head. We often answer more fully and honestly because we can't take the easy route of avoiding a question which will stretch us in some way.

"'Someday' is a disease that will take your dreams
to the grave with you."
Tim Ferris

Make it easier to leave your old role

When you're planning how you will move from one job to the next, you may think briefly about who'll deliver your job when you move. While this may not seem like your responsibility, this thinking, known as succession planning, can be helpful to you achieving your move.

Succession planning is about ensuring the right competencies, (for example, skills, knowledge, experience, and behaviours) are available in the people who will be helping an organisation meet its goals. Managers need to be aware that their team members can change jobs for all sorts of reasons so, to keep an organisation running effectively, it's important to plan ahead and make sure a source of the right competencies will be available when someone moves out of a role.

Perhaps you are asking yourself 'Why do I need to do my own succession planning?' Because if there is no-one ready to do your job, your manager may feel less enthusiastic about taking steps to help you move on. Being indispensable can sound like a good thing on some occasions, this just isn't one of them.

As you create your plan to become ready-now for your next role, take a look around you and decide how easily your manager could find a replacement for you.

To help your manager feel more enthusiastic about helping you move on, here are steps you can take to oil the wheels.

- Knowing what you know about your role, decide who would make a good replacement for you
- Take the opportunity to share tips or skills for your role with potential candidates for your replacement. The closer they are to being ready to do your role, the easier your move will feel to your manager
- Be prepared to offer your manager some suggestions for who you feel could do your role effectively. This may be someone inside the organisation, or it may be someone you know outside the organisation
- When you consider someone you know who could be suitable to fill your role, make a note of which competencies they already have, and which they will need to develop to be equipped to do the role. Your manager will want to build their own opinion of this, but a few clues from the person currently doing the job can make a welcome starting point

Launch your plan

By now you'll be feeling more confident and eager to be proactive about reaching your next development goal. Great! Use that confidence now to begin.

Take the first steps on your plan and continue from there. As you continue, make regular time for a little reflection on how things are going. Pop a reminder in your calendar once every two months or more frequently if change is occurring quickly. Use these moments to briefly check the three P's: Purpose, Plan and Progress.

To check purpose, go back to what you decided you want to create in life and work and check these are still important to you. Have relationships changed? Have job opportunities changed? Has your experience of your role or your interest in future roles changed what you're looking for?

German military strategist Helmuth von Moltke's famous quote "No battle plan survives contact with the enemy" advises us to regularly compare our plan with the evolving real-world around us, and adjust it for any changes so it remains fit for our purpose.

You'll discover which way of reviewing progress works best for you. A good approach is to note the progress you have made along the stages and outcomes in your plan, and blend this assessment with feedback you request from others. Learn from your successes, and from anything that was not so successful, so you are better prepared for the next stage in your plan.

Remember to develop your skills, knowledge and behaviours in a way which fits with your personal values and integrity. Enjoy developing yourself and do so in a way that makes you even more comfortable in being you. Go, do it now!

"Did you live, did you love fully?
Did you make a difference, did you matter?"
Brendon Burchard

Chapter review

After building your plan, take the time to reflect on what you've discovered by using the following questions.

Building your plan

- What have you learned from building your personal plan?
- Where will you start?
- Who can help you launch your plan?
- Who are your potential successors?
- What else will drive you to put thought into action?

Part II

It's all about my staff

The first section of this book is designed to help you when you want to change your own job. This second section will appeal to you if you are a team leader, a manager, project manager or a senior leader wanting tips on how to support your staff in their progression from being ready-later to being ready-now.

This section will also be valuable to you when you have a manager or one or more stakeholders, because it reveals the secrets of how they could be supporting you.

22

Why encourage my staff to take a new role?

Motivated staff

In the section Approaching the gaps : Keep motivated on page 69, you will have read about FLOW, and how we humans feel more confident, motivated, and less stressed when we are in FLOW, having a reasonable balance between the level of challenge we are presented with, and the level of capability we have to meet that challenge.

Supporting the development of an individual provides them with new opportunities to maintain FLOW, and to the reap the benefits that brings.

The risks of not supporting your staff with their progression are:

a) They reach a level where their capability to do their existing role exceeds the challenge of the role

b) They gradually become less motivated and bored

c) Their performance drops

d) Their attitude starts to negatively affect the work of colleagues around them

e) They start to look for fresh challenges outside the role, outside the employer, or in the worst case, they lose their motivation completely and suffer physiological health issues as a result

If the list needs one more entry to convince you, here it is: as a manager, you are accountable for supporting your staff with their development.

Your direct reports have a choice; to develop themselves and seek further opportunities, or not. Their choice will have implications not just for themselves, but for you and your organisation.

As a manager your accountability is to encourage them to develop, and to have the adult-adult conversation with them about the positive benefits of personal development and any negative implications of making the choice not to.

"Train people well enough so they can leave but treat them well enough so they don't want to."
Richard Branson

Preparing for the future

By carefully supporting your staff in their development, you can maintain a motivating level of challenge in their role, which encourages them to be productive. Your support can also contribute to your succession planning for the organisation.

There is always a risk that an individual will move, and this could be due to a wide variety of reasons, some of which you will have no influence over. A little succession planning and personal development planning can help you decide how you will fill their position if they do leave.

Perhaps the answer is as simple as posting a vacancy on an online recruiting site. That is one way of bringing in some fresh opinions and ideas. But you may want to fill the position with someone who already knows the role, knows the culture, knows how you like the work done, and who you feel fits with your organisation. One way of planning for this is to have a succession development plan, deciding who is ready-now or could be ready-later to fill each role. If there are roles for which only ready-later candidates are available, you can decide how to work with them so they fill the gaps to become ready-now.

Chapter review

Use the following questions to reflect on your role of encouraging staff to develop.

Why encourage them to take a new role?

- What are you currently doing to encourage your staff to think about their next role (or their next challenge within their role) and develop towards it?
- How successful have you been in achieving this?
- What more will you do now?

23

Having the discussion about being ready-later

How often have you heard someone talk about a future opportunity they have been offered, but the opportunity never seems to materialise. They are told:

"The timing isn't right."

"There are other priorities."

"We need to make sure a few more things are in place."

"We need your skills where you are."

"You're very close, but this time we're going to give the opportunity to someone else."

These are real-world examples, and you may have overheard similar yourself.

But how would hearing these motivate you if you heard them time and time again?

As a manager, it's your accountability and responsibility to listen to the aspirations of your staff, and to help them understand the brutal facts of the current situation and the future opportunities.

When someone is within reach of being ready-now

When you have a discussion with someone who you feel is within reach of being described as ready-now for a role, we describe them as being ready-later. When you talk to someone who you feel will be ready-later for a role, be brutally clear about the strengths they need to maintain, and equally about the gaps they need to fill, to move along the path from being ready-later to being ready-now. Have an adult-adult conversation with them. Give them the facts, so they have the freedom to make a choice about whether they are willing to work on maintaining the relevant strengths, and whether they are motivated to fill the required gaps.

You will find an essential guide for how to have an adult-to-adult conversation in the section Have 'adult to adult' conversations on page 227.

The meaning of 'within reach' of being ready-now

Before you make a decision positively or negatively that someone is 'within reach' of being ready-now you'll need to back up your decision with some reasonable criteria.
At a summary level, here are two criteria we recommend including:

- Is there a high probability you can create a realistic development plan, which the staff member can accomplish, so they can fill the gaps to become ready-now within 18 months?

- Is there a high probability there will be a suitable role available at the time the individual will be ready? Use your judgement. Apply what you know about availability within and outside the organisation.

If there is not a realistic probability of them being ready-now within 18 months, or you don't expect a role to be available in that time, be honest about it and don't tell them they'll be ready-later.

When someone is not within reach of being ready-now

When someone is not within reach of being ready-now for a role they are interested in, it's time for a conversation to talk clearly about the facts, even though you may feel the facts are brutal to discuss. Be honest about the reasons for your opinion and be specific. Lead the discussion about the implications of not being within reach, and describe alternative opportunities, so your employee truly knows what roles are, and aren't available.

Knowing these facts may be uncomfortable for your staff member, but it allows them to make an informed choice about their future direction. Explain clearly that providing them with this choice is your purpose. If you cloud the facts, you're deciding not to give them the freedom of choice.

"I have a development opportunity for you"

A client recently complained to us "I've just been given *another* development opportunity by my boss." He used his fingers to mime speech marks around the words 'development opportunity'. "Every time he needs me to do something different he calls it a development opportunity. To start with I was fine with it. I assumed he was giving me opportunities which would add up to something. But now I realise that isn't true."

When you use the phrase 'development opportunity,' use it sparingly and meaningfully. Follow these rules:

Be honest about the opportunity: If it's not really an opportunity for the person to develop, in a direction which they will recognise as helpful, don't call it a development opportunity. Just explain there is something you need them to do. If you realise this really is a development opportunity, but you have not discussed this specific need for their development before, then take a moment to have that conversation right way.

Be explicit about the development: Be explicit about which part of the opportunity is the source of their development; the challenge for them. Give your staff member a way of measuring what success looks like in this development area, so they know what to aim for and whether they are on target. Be precise in what you want them to develop and how. If you are not clear and precise, how can they be expected to know what to do differently? Without clarity and precision, how can they fully benefit from the opportunity and demonstrate their progress or growth?

Explain the purpose of the development opportunity: Connect the challenge in the development opportunity with the purpose of giving it to your direct report. For example, the challenge may be to maintain or encourage FLOW for them because they have become very competent in other activities they do. The challenge may be to develop skills, knowledge and behaviours which help to fill their gaps between being ready-later and ready-now for a role. Alternatively, the challenge may help them develop into being fully competent in all aspects of their existing role.

By following these rules, your offer of a 'development opportunity' will be genuine and meaningful.

Chapter review

Use the following questions to reflect on how you will improve your discussions about being ready-later.

Having the discussion about ready-later

- Which of your staff can be described as ready-later for their next role?
- Which staff can be described as ready-now?
- Who do you find is easy to overlook?
- Who will benefit from a real development opportunity?
- Who needs to know they are *not* going to be ready for their next role during the next 18 months?
- What opportunities do you have for using straight facts to help give someone the freedom of choice?

24

How to help a staff member become ready-now

Do you know someone who you regard as ready-later for a role, and for whom you need to provide some support? Or is that a situation you can imagine occurring in the future? Whatever the timing for you, you'll want to be aware of good practice, and then decide for yourself what you'll do. In the next few chapters, we'll describe how you can prepare yourself to give them your support, plus solid, effective tools you can use to help them.

25

Understanding your staff

Check your assumptions

We all carry a set of assumptions and presuppositions about how the world is and how it works. These are generally helpful to us and allow us to get through our day in a more effective and more efficient way. Imagine a world in which you do not carry these around. Every morning as you brush your teeth you'd have to work out which end of the toothbrush to hold, where to put the toothpaste and even which motion to use. It would be a frustrating start to the day wouldn't it? Now multiply that frustration by every action you carry out during the day. Life would become impossible.

So, assumptions can be helpful, but we can be caught out by our assumptions too. Have you ever found yourself striding briskly towards a door and reached your hand out to push it open, only to find yourself coming to a sudden stop? Somehow, you ignored a sign which clearly said 'pull'. There was something about that door which fired your assumption that pushing was the right action to take.

These assumptions and presuppositions are internal rules we've discovered work well enough to be adopted by us, but they may not be the same for everyone. A colleague of ours was surprised to read about our door example and, looking puzzled, asked us "Are you telling me you don't just look for the door hinge on every door? If you can see the hinge, you can assume the door opens towards you." He was using a very different assumption.

Assumptions about people

In the same way, we can carry assumptions and presuppositions about the people around us. These are often based on surprisingly little data. Our assumption may be based on a single interaction, conversation or piece of feedback. They may even be based on what we've been told by other people.

When you're planning the personal development of a staff member, be aware that you run the risk of making assumptions about them which could drive the wrong development decisions.

In making assumptions about how competent they are, you could be assuming they are great, good, average, poor or very poor. That's a one in five chance of being correct. Not good odds.

One risk is you assume they have more capability than they possess, and encourage them into a role which is too much for them. This will be stressful and demoralising for them personally and the organisation suffers from their poor performance.

Another risk is to assume they have a lower capability than they possess, and overlook them when new opportunities emerge. This is frustrating for the individual and a missed opportunity for the organisation.

As human beings, we're also biased to like people who are like us. As managers, if we follow this bias we'll develop and recruit the employees who are most like ourselves. Not a good tactic when research tells us that diversity in organisations drives creativity, innovation and strong performance.

Fair development of your staff

As a manager, you have a responsibility for the fair development of your staff. For all of the reasons above, it's important you take the time to become aware of your assumptions and check them before acting on them.

When you're planning someone's development, a good place to start is to pull out the last assessment you made of their capabilities and performance. Re-read it or, if you don't have an assessment already, write an assessment of their stronger and weaker attributes. Put the assessment to one side, and review it a few days later with some critical thinking. Ask yourself what hard evidence supports each of your statements. When you find a point with weak or insufficient evidence, take action to gather sufficient evidence to satisfy the most critical person you can think of.

Once you're satisfied the assessment is robust from your point of view, ask someone else to help you test your assessment. Ask them to review it with you, and ask you supportive, critical questions about the reasons for your opinions. You'll find this step very enlightening.

Having verified your assessment, and talked to your employee to check what else you might be assuming, you'll be able to proceed with a much higher degree of confidence in your chosen course of action.

Understanding different communications styles and how they can help a manager

In Part I, you'll have read about how we communicate most easily with people who have a similar communication style to ourselves (see Building rapport using awareness of communication styles on page 90). What does this mean for you in your role as a manager?

Knowing we communicate most easily with people who communicate like us can have a range of implications when you are planning the development of your staff:

- The potential for you to have a positive bias towards some employees, those who communicate in a similar way to yourself, and negative bias towards others
- The risk you ignore or discount useful information because it's presented to you in someone else's communication style, not matching yours
- The risk you communicate the allocation of tasks in a way which is natural for you but more difficult for others to absorb in a positive way
- The potential to miss the strengths of having diversity in your organisation, because you only hire those who communicate like you

As a reminder, our personal style of communication can be identified by the level of 'asking' or 'telling' we use, and by the amount of emotion we use.

The four communication styles

Communicate with low emotion

Asking style of communication

Analytic style	Driving style
Amiable style	Expressive style

Telling style of communication

Communicate with high emotion

Those who prefer low emotion and a telling style are referred to as having a Driving preference. They are often people who control their emotions and speak assertively. They prefer to control a situation and are focused on big-picture results. Others may see them as highly delivery-focused, wanting to get the job done, but without concern for relationships or feelings.

Those who have a preference for a telling style, and also a degree of emotion, are said to have an Expressive preference. These people show their emotions and speak assertively. They enjoy sharing their ideas and perspectives openly with others. Others may see them as creative, but unfocused.

Those with a more asking preference, and who communicate with emotion have an Amiable preference. These people show their emotions openly and prefer to ask questions rather than give orders. Relationships, feelings and personal security are important to them. Others may see them as friendly but spend too much time talking.

The final group is of people who use an asking preference with lower emotion. These have an Analytic preference. These people control their emotions but tend to ask questions rather than give orders. They are focused on tasks and accuracy, and they act deliberately to achieve that end. Others may see them as slow-paced and detail-oriented.

Each style has its own set of priorities guiding which is most important: maintaining relationships, or completing tasks, and each style has its own pace of how fast things should be done.

Those with a Driver style or Expressive style tend to prefer a faster pace, while those with an Amiable style or Analytical style tend to prefer a slower pace.

How people with one communication style see others with a different style

To help you identify and overcome any potential bias in favour of those who communicate like you, the following table illustrates assumptions you may have made, simply because of communication style differences. Remember, this works in reverse too. Your staff may well have made assumptions about you, based on your communication style.

This information is helpful when working with others, and also useful to know when you are hiring new staff or forming a team, so you can encourage diversity.

Your Preference	Other's preference	How you may see the other person
Driving	Driving	Efficient, effective, hard working
	Expressive	Easily excited, emotional, wastes time
	Analytic	Slow paced, unnecessarily worried about getting all the data. Hard to get a direct answer from them
	Amiable	Never delivers anything, spends far too much time worrying about how people may feel. Spends a lot of time talking

Your Preference	Other's preference	How you may see the other person
Expressive	Driving	Good pace but rather cold and uncaring. Don't seem to have any passion for the important things
	Expressive	Great to be with. Generate really exciting and creative work together even when we disagree
	Analytic	Slow paced, unexciting, hard to work with. Seem to need lots of information rather than just getting on with things. Very difficult to get an opinion from them
	Amiable	Nice people but rather hesitant and slow to get on with the work

Your preference	Other's preference	How you may see the other person
Analytic	Driving	Push on with things even when the data doesn't support them. Pushy and domineering
	Expressive	Excessively emotional. Doesn't act on facts, just jumps in and takes action without thinking about it
	Analytic	Professional people who take the right amount of time thinking about things and making sure they have the right amount of data before acting
	Amiable	OK people but share unnecessary emotions and feelings. Talk too much. Uninterested in facts and details

Your Preference	Other's preference	How you may see the other person
Amiable	Driving	Unnecessarily pushy and uncaring. Only ever interested in the task with no feeling for the people at all
	Expressive	Rush in and are too excitable, but caring underneath it all
	Analytic	Rather cold and too focused on the data. Uninterested in relationships
	Amiable	Very caring, supportive people to be around

Communication styles and staff development

You may have recognised your own preference from this overview of communication styles. Perhaps you've recognised a difference in preferences as the reason you find communication with some of your staff difficult. They may also be struggling with their communication with you for the same reason. It's worth repeating that it's very easy to negatively judge people with a different preference from your own, and to form an incorrect assessment of them and their capability.

During development reviews and planning, as well as in day-to-day activities, bear in mind your own preferences and those of your employees.

Develop your own communication style flexibility so you can sprinkle a bit of their style into your communication. Do this by simply strengthening the amount of your 'ask' or 'tell' to more closely match their preference for a while. Similarly regulate the amount of emotion you use to match their preference.

Even small adjustments can have a positive impact. For example, when an Analytic preferenced staff member increases the level of 'tell' during a conversation with a leader who has a strong Driving preference, the leader will unconsciously find the exchange more to their liking. They will find it easier to absorb what they are hearing.

Encourage your staff to practise this flexibility too, to allow them to work better with others and successfully influence others.

Understanding what they really want

Among all the gifts you have received in the past, it is likely that at least one has caused you surprise. Perhaps because the gift giver was so adamant about it matching you perfectly, but when you opened it, you felt grateful, but didn't know why they selected it for you.

On reflection, you may have realised they chose something which they would have really liked themselves. They were trying to do their best for you by giving you something they would have enjoyed. Their intent was perfect, but it isn't right for you because you aren't them.

In the same way, people are offered career opportunities which don't work for them. Their manager may have worked very hard to create the opportunity but, because it doesn't fit, they are faced with an employee who isn't showing the expected enthusiasm and gratitude. That can be disappointing for a manager.

So, what's gone wrong?

Usually the primary cause is an assumption. Either the manager assumes they know what the employee wants, or they have assumed they know what will work for the employee because it has worked for them in their own career.

The great news is you can avoid this situation with a few simple steps.

1. Ask them what they want – This may sound blindingly obvious, but it is amazing how frequently this step is either missed out or carried out superficially.

2. Listen carefully to the answer and repeat back what you have heard to make sure you have understood what they actually meant, not just what you *thought* they meant.

3. Identify what you are still unclear about. Use precision questions to draw out more from their descriptions; you can boost your precision questioning skills by following the tips in the chapter Gap: I need to improve finding out facts and details on page 105. Using these questions will not only check your understanding, but also encourage them to decide what they mean in sufficient detail. Asking questions can even liberate new thinking from them and will ensure you have a common understanding, and can progress with confidence.

4. Ask some questions to understand whether what they are asking for matches with their higher goals. Using the simple question "And when you have that, what will it give you?" will be very helpful. By asking this, waiting for the answer and then asking it again a couple of times, you'll draw out the connection between what they want and their larger goals, and really build their motivation to be successful in achieving it.

5. Remember, the person in front of you is not you. They have their own history, preferences, needs and desires. This may mean you need to ask them about their communication preferences, their learning styles (See section I, Fine-tuning how you learn, to learn more effectively on page 73) and their domestic circumstances as you jointly develop ideas for their future career opportunities. If you feel curious about how they'll feel about answering these questions, simply start by explaining the reason you want to ask the question, and then ask if they feel it's acceptable to talk about that subject.

Chapter review

Reflect on the following questions to challenge yourself and to decide what you will do differently knowing all you have learned from this chapter.

Understanding your staff

- What assumptions might you be carrying about each of your staff members?
- What do you need to do to check these assumptions?
- What are the risks if you continue with some of your unchecked assumptions?
- What steps will you take to avoid making new assumptions about your staff from now on?
- What is your preferred communication style?
    - With whom will you flex your communication style to generate a more productive conversation?
- What personal development do each of your staff members really want, and what is their purpose for wanting the development?
    - If you don't know, what will you do to find out?

26

Improving poor performance

There may be occasions when you are managing someone whose behaviour, or performance in a particular activity, is not what you or they would want it to be. In these cases, you need a strategy to help them improve. Experience tells us that, during a performance review, simply saying "You need to be better at ….." rarely if ever leads to improved performance. So you need to understand what might be happening and what to do about it.

When we talk to managers about improving an individual's performance, we ask them to start with two thought-provoking assumptions and one important check:

Assumption 1: Very few people deliberately set out to be poor performers at work. In our experience, most people come to work to do a good job and to receive a fair reward for their work.

Assumption 2: People always make the best choices from the alternatives they perceive are available to them at the time. By available we mean the choice is possible and the individual knows the choice exists and believes they can choose to do it.

Make a final check before deciding you are dealing with poor performance. Ask yourself these questions:

- Does the individual know what is expected of them? How do they describe it?
- Have they been given the right resources to do the role?

With these assumptions in mind, and assuming you will have made the check, it's time to explore a common cause of poor performance.

Before you do, remember the poor performance may be restricted to specific activities and behaviours, so be precise in how you talk about any poor performance. Saying "Randall is a poor performer" tells a very different story when compared with "Randall's performance is poor during the final 30 minutes of sales calls each Friday."

A common cause of poor performance

While coaching individuals who have shown poor performance, we usually find, at some level, they are operating with negative expectations of what they can achieve. This causes them to limit their own performance, often unconsciously. They've become stuck in the cycle of negative expectations shown in the following picture.

The cycle and impact of negative expectations

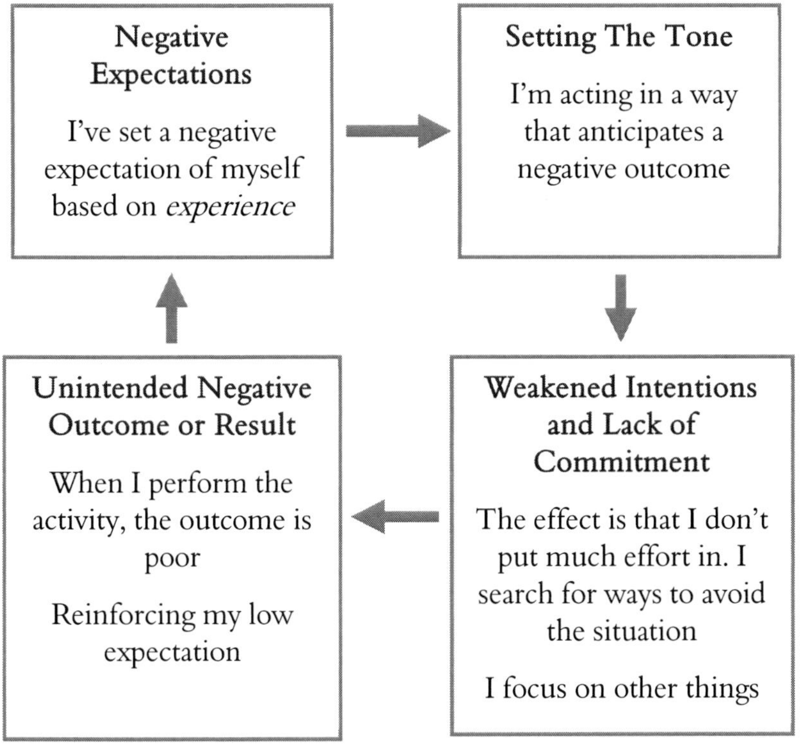

- Medium and low performers find a past bad experience has set a negative expectation for similar activities in the future.
- The individual then acts in a way which anticipates a negative outcome.
- Those actions lead to a lack of commitment to achieve the outcome.
- This, in turn, leads to a negative or unachieved result which reinforces the negative expectation for the future.

An example will help illustrate this cycle.

A client, Mary, contacted us because she felt unable to make a presentation to a group of people, a limitation which was becoming unhelpful to her career. She wasn't alone in having this limitation.

When Mary was asked how long she had felt this way, she remembered a specific occasion several years previously when she had given a presentation. She told us "A colleague said he was disappointed with my presentation, which left me feeling embarrassed and awkward and very unwilling to do any more."

After that experience Mary explained "I avoided making presentations and on the few occasions when I couldn't avoid it, I knew I was going to make a mess of it again and, guess what, I was right. I still hate doing them. I seem to under prepare or over prepare or do something else wrong."

This is a real example of the negative expectations cycle and its impact. Mary's poor feedback experience caused her to build a negative expectation and act in a way that anticipated a negative outcome at future presentations. In turn, this led to her acting in a way that avoided the situation, avoiding presentations when she could and passing the opportunity to other people.

When avoiding wasn't an option Mary described her subsequent presentation delivery as hesitant, reading off the slides to keep to the point and, overall, she painted a picture of someone with low confidence. She remembered looking at her audience: "I was worried they were bored and my presenting was simply ineffective." The feedback she received echoed this and reinforced her belief she couldn't do presentations to a group of people.

Perhaps you have talked to someone who has similar worries, or negative expectations, about 'doing maths', using computers, cooking, revising, handling stress, or playing a sport.

Often, all they need is a kick-start to help them jump out of the negative expectation cycle and move on.

This kick-start may be as simple as asking them a couple of questions, questions which can unlock the cycle and transform medium or low performance into high performance.

So how can you provide a kick start? The following diagram shows the steps you can take to get things moving.

How To Improve Expectations

1 Identify
Notice the individual has negative or low expectations

2 Challenge
Challenge the expectations.
Use precision questions.
Check assumptions

3 Decision
Encourage individual to decide if they want to change their default expectations

4 New Expectations
Encourage new, positive expectations from the individual

5 Plan
Encourage individual to develop a plan, with outcomes, to achieve success

6 Pre-launch Checks
Ask individual to step through the plan. Check the success will be achieved

Here's how it works:

- First, you must become aware that the individual's expectations are low. The clues can be simple to find, phrases such as "I'm no good at presentations", "They would never want to hear my ideas", "I always freeze when I'm in front of senior managers" or "I can't find the right words quickly in a discussion" are clear indicators. The clues are often expressed as generalisations or absolute rules and are always negative.

- Next, challenge the generalisations with precision questions or by testing the assumptions being made. For example: "What precisely do you mean by no good?"

- Once you have some precision, ask the individual if they are willing to change the situation. This is important. In saying they are willing to change they give themselves permission to change. If they are unwilling to make a change, tell them the implications of that decision, and discuss the available options for what will happen next.

- If they are willing to make a change, you now encourage them to set new, positive expectations. Ask them to prepare for the next occasion (for example, the next presentation) by thinking about the occasion as if it had gone very well and by describing how it went, vividly and very positively.

- Work with them to define the steps they need to take to ensure the next occasion will meet this new positive expectation.

- Finally, ask them to talk through their steps and, once they have done this, check how their confidence has improved. If they are not yet approaching the situation positively, it may be necessary to build in a few extra steps to further strengthen their confidence and check again.

Remember, once the individual has successfully delivered the plan and achieved success, you have a fantastic opportunity to reinforce their success by either praising them yourself, or by collecting feedback for them to use as positive reinforcement.

Take encouragement from sportsman Michael Jordan who said:

"If you accept the expectations of others, especially negative ones, then you never will change the outcome."

This is even more true when we listen to our own 'self-talk', our inner monologue.

The expectations we set in our heads overrule everything someone else tells us, which is why successful sports women and men work carefully to 'get their head in the game' before they compete. They make sure to have a motivating expectation in their mind.

Helping someone to change their negative expectations can be one of the greatest gifts you can give them, so look out for the opportunity and take action.

Chapter review

Reflect on the following questions to challenge yourself and to decide what you will do differently knowing all you have learned from reading this chapter.

Improving poor performance

- Who in your staff may be hindered by negative expectations?
- How will you find out?
- What are you going to do to help?
- What conversations do you need to have?
- Who could assist you?

27

Do what you usually do – but with more impact

Many managers tell us they are already taking some steps to develop their staff to become ready-now for their next role and, while they'd like to do more, they can't always find the time. They want to know how they can get even more impact from the time they are currently investing in supporting this development.

So, how can you radically improve the impact of your support while doing the activities you normally do? Here are our tips for a tune-up.

28

Power up your feedback giving

It's often been said feedback is a gift to the recipient. However, while many managers spend significant time and thought preparing and delivering their feedback, they discover it doesn't always have the effect they want and some don't give it at all.

Firstly, do give feedback. A 2009 Gallup poll assessing the impact of manager feedback on employee engagement reported that managers giving little or no feedback failed to engage 98% of their staff. They found that even poor feedback was better than no feedback, but set your sights higher than that.

We recommend the following ways to make sure you get the positive effect you intend from your feedback:

- Thank people routinely. Look for the opportunity to thank and praise people with the same level of rigour you look for opportunities for improvement.

- Reflect for a moment on what kind of conversations you have with your staff routinely. When your staff see you, do you ask them about what's going well and what they can learn from that, or do you ask them what problems they are handling and what they are doing about them? When you find something going well remember to thank your staff for the work they have done or are doing.

- Be precise with your feedback. Be specific about exactly when, where and what you are giving feedback about, and what specifically the person has done well or could improve and how.

- To help someone consider a new role or opportunity during a development discussion build their confidence by recognising what they have already achieved. Then relate it to the new opportunity. For example: "This new role is something you could do because of your skills and experience in catering, and we could support you picking up the extra skills for managing customer relationships."

Give 'towards' feedback

Spend your time focusing on what the person should be doing, rather than on what they shouldn't. Focus on helping them move toward the next role rather than away from what they are currently doing. To do this effectively you'll need to describe what you are asking them to do precisely, in positive terms. Some examples of vague, away from statements and more precise, towards statements can be found in the following table.

Poor precision, 'away from' statement	How to improve precision	Precise example. A forward looking, 'towards' statement
You aren't visible enough.	What is meant by visible? Visible to who? Visible doing what?	You need to make three sales presentations, in front of Mike, which lead to new customers signing up to our support contract.
You aren't experienced enough.	Experienced in what? How much experience is required?	You need to spend 24 months working in a project management role and deliver 2 projects with a total value of over 4 million dollars.

Poor precision, away from statement	How to improve precision	Precise example. A forward looking, 'towards' statement
You don't have enough international experience	How much is enough? What is meant by international experience?	You need to work on at least one 12-month secondment in Asia Pacific. It doesn't matter what role precisely but it must be at career band E or above.
You work isn't good enough quality.	What work specifically? What is meant by better quality? For how long does this need to be done to demonstrate competence?	You need to produce deviation reports which are accepted first time 95% of the time for a 6-month period before we can consider moving you to the next role.

Chapter review

Reflect on the following questions to challenge yourself and to decide what you will do differently knowing all you have learned from reading this chapter.

Power up your feedback giving

- How precise is your feedback?
- How consistent are you in using a 'towards' approach when you give guidance and feedback?
- What feedback would benefit your reports?
- What are you going to do differently in your frequency and approach to giving feedback?
- What feedback would benefit you and when will you ask for it?

29

Be agile in your support and challenge

Have you ever asked someone a question you hoped was going to be helpful and supportive, and the reaction you received made you feel you had really critically challenged them? Or perhaps you wanted to challenge someone to think differently and their reaction made you feel as though you had simply agreed with them.

The reaction we receive to our questions is never guaranteed, but we can improve the odds by being measured in the amount of support compared to the amount of creative challenge we inject into our questions.

Flexing the level of support and challenge will draw out new ideas and understanding, and encourage new thinking about existing ideas and decisions. By getting the balance right it's possible to encourage good performance, personal development and growth. Often, as this positive progress occurs, it can be helpful to increase the level of challenge and help someone to develop into a further, higher level of performance.

The first tip for developing this flexibility of support and challenge is to appreciate that the approach you use will be tuned to match the person you are talking to.

As a manager, it is important to recognise the effect of your challenge and support will vary depending on the wider context of the support and challenge the individual is experiencing in their life situation. The amount of support and challenge you use must match their situation. This is not a 'one size fits all' approach, but happily, if you are aware of the basic principles and follow our simple tips, you will discover how to instantly develop that match.

Principle 1: Balance can encourage personal performance. For our best, sustained, personal performance we need some level of balance between the amount of support we receive and the amount of challenge we receive. Like many aspects of life, too much of one thing is not healthy for us.

The effect of varying levels of support and creative challenge on performance

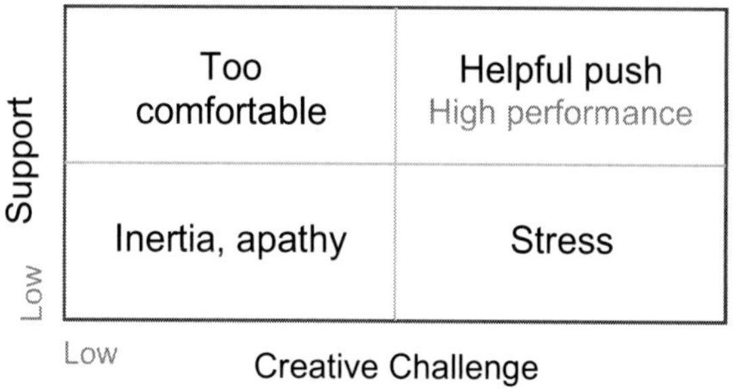

Support ↑	Low Creative Challenge →	
High	Too comfortable	Helpful push High performance
Low	Inertia, apathy	Stress

Support (Low) / Creative Challenge (Low)

Challenging Coaching: Jon Blakey & Ian Day

Too much support: In athletics, the coach or trainer has the job of helping a sprinter reach their full potential. Imagine then if the trainer *only* used supportive conversations. For example, "So you were last again, but I'm sure you enjoyed the exercise and your new running shoes looked great!" or "You are about to start the new season so let's wait and see what happens this year" or "Your lap time today was a little over 2 minutes. It's interesting that sometimes you run faster, sometimes slower. I like it!"

Added together, and repeated, these phrases would encourage the athlete to become too comfortable. The words don't encourage them to develop their talent and, without another source of challenge, the athlete would be very unlikely to reach their full potential.

Too much challenge: When Jo, a friend ours, signed up to a gym to increase her fitness, the advisor provided her with a list of weekly exercises. She discovered the first week's exercises were not highly challenging. When she asked about the level of challenge in them he replied:

"I've some exercises in there you'll do easily and there are some which will challenge you a little, but they're all within reach of what you could achieve today. If I gave you a list of killer exercises for your first week, you'd hurt, you'd feel you weren't making progress, it would be too much too soon, and I'd probably never see you here again."

He understood the right level of challenge would motivate her to continue at the gym, and gradually improve, while an excessive level of challenge would have switched off her motivation. It worked, and she's been motivated to gradually raise the level of challenge so she enjoys her fitness regime.

If we're repeatedly given very challenging tasks at work, with insufficient knowledge and resources to do them, and no help or acknowledgement for what we *do* achieve then we quickly become stressed and our performance drops below our best.

Low support and low challenge: Where there are very few challenges and little support this encourages apathy, a don't-care attitude, an inertia and resistance to change.

Balanced medium to high levels of challenge and support: A good balance of active support and challenge provides a 'helpful push' which stimulates high performance. In athletics, we'd expect to hear the trainer using a balance, for example:

"Your target's 2 minutes, you achieved 2 minutes 5 seconds so you're close. You've improved by 3 seconds today. Good job. Now let's lock in that improvement while we work on cutting out the next 3 seconds."

Principle 2: Environment affects perceived levels of support and challenge. How we perceive a question, as challenging or supportive, is very personal to each of us, and depends on what's happening around us at that time. If you are in a situation which is already very challenging and stressful then a question with a seemingly low level of challenge, such as "How soon can I have the result?" can

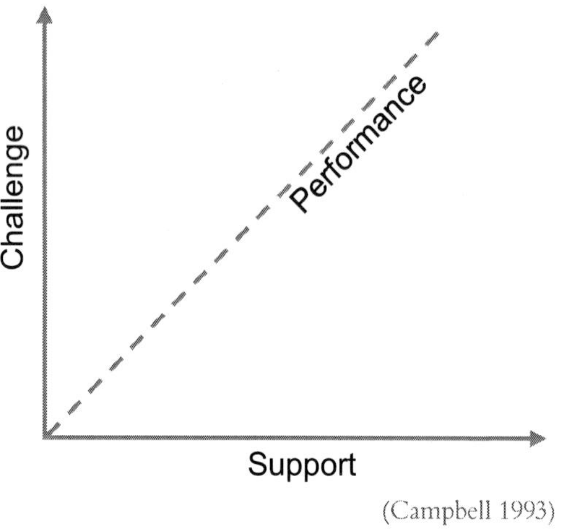

(Campbell 1993)

feel like a much stronger challenge because you are already stressed.

If someone is used to a very supportive environment where all they hear is good news, a simple supportive question like "I'm curious, what will be different when this is completed" can feel like a challenge because they are not used to being asked for an explanation.

In summary then, remember the person who ultimately judges the level of support or challenge in what you say is not you. It's the person you are talking to, and they are judging it based on their reaction to what is happening in their environment at that time.

Principle 3: You can tune your support and challenge questions to match the individual.

We all have our own preferences for how we think and how we communicate. To ask a supportive question, take care to match the preferences of the person you are talking to. To ask a challenging question, create a mismatch between your question and the individual's preferences. How to do this is explained in the following tips.

Tips for creating supportive or creatively challenging questions

Use the following tips to develop your flexibility in adding support or creative challenge to your conversations. We use the term 'creatively' challenging because the objective of these challenges is to encourage new ideas and future-thinking, to encourage an acknowledgement of the brutal facts of a situation so the starting point for any decision is clear, and to develop a solid foundation of confidence on which further personal development will build. The supportive and creative challenge are both essential tools in encouraging high performance from ourselves and those we talk to.

Tip 1: Noticing how someone prefers to talk

To tune your questions specifically to the person you are talking to, take a moment to observe how the person usually talks, i.e. their preferences for how they communicate.

- Do they spend more time telling people information, or do they spend more time asking questions?
- Do they share their emotions and feelings as they talk, or do they stick to facts and information?
- Do they talk about what's happening now, or what things will be like in the future?
- Do they talk about the purpose of things or concentrate on the detail?
- Do they talk about assumptions or facts?
- Do they talk about the size of the challenges or the level of capability available to meet a challenge?

Tip 2: How to be more Supportive

Always build early rapport in a conversation by asking questions which match the preferences of the person you are talking to.

To continue the conversation in a supportive style, maintain the match between your questions and the preference of the person you are talking to.

Here are examples of supportive questions, matched to the preference of the person you are talking to.

Their preference	What they said	Your supportive question (matching their preference)
Sticking to facts	The trains are at 11am, 1pm and 4pm and one of them is an express train	What time do you need to arrive? What's the most you want to pay for your ticket?
Sharing emotions	I'm feeling confused about all the train times available and stressed about which to choose	Which train time will give you the confidence you will arrive in good time and feeling relaxed?
Spending more time 'telling'	The interviews have *got* to be done on Tuesday	What *must* you do to make that happen?
Spending more time 'asking'	I'm wondering if the interviews should be on Tuesday?	What could you do to make that happen?
Talking about what is happening now	I'm worried about how I'll organise the project report	What experience of your previous reports can you build on?
Talking about the future	When all stages are completed I'll start to relax	Which stages will have been the most important?

Use the following to make your question more supportive:

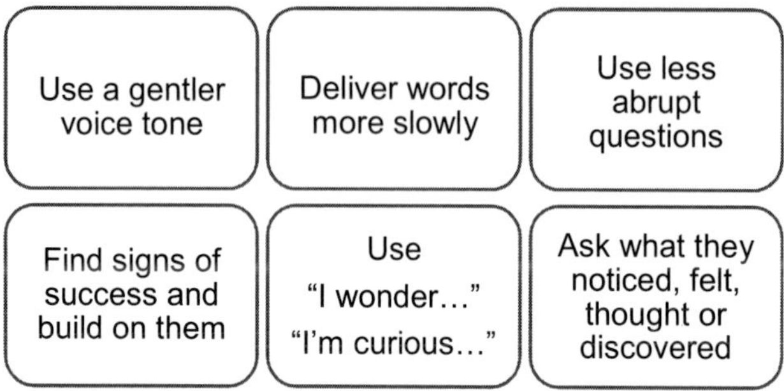

Use a gentler voice tone
Deliver words more slowly
Use less abrupt questions
Find signs of success and build on them
Use "I wonder…" "I'm curious…"
Ask what they noticed, felt, thought or discovered

Tip 3: How to be more creatively challenging

To move to a more creatively challenging style, ask questions which do not match the style of the person you are talking to *plus* start by signalling the purpose behind your question. Signalling the purpose behind your question is a great way of making challenging questions become more creative and acceptable because the listener hears the context of the question first, rather than having to guess the reason for you asking. If you know someone who regularly responds defensively when you ask them a question, the technique of signalling your purpose behind the question before asking it can help reduce that defensiveness. Assuming, of course, the purpose behind your question resonates well with them.

The following are examples of creatively challenging questions matched to the other person's preference:

Their preference	What they said	Your creatively challenging question (doesn't match their preference)
Sticking to facts	The trains are at 11am, 1pm and 4pm and one of them is an express train	So that you arrive feeling relaxed, which train are you confident will get you there in good time?
Sharing emotions	I'm feeling confused about all the train times available and stressed about which to choose	So you can get this decided, what time do you need to arrive and how long does the journey take?
Spending more time 'telling'	The interviews have got to be done on Tuesday	To help fit this with other priorities I'm curious what makes Tuesday so attractive, when we have spare time on Friday?
Spending more time 'asking'	I'm wondering if the interviews should be on Tuesday?	To help fit this with other priorities convince me: why Tuesday?
Talking about what is happening now	I'm worried about how I'll organise the project report	To get you started, which three sections will your customer most want to read?
Talking about the future	When all stages are completed I'll start to relax	So I know where we are now, which stages are most complete today?

Use the following to make your questions more challenging:

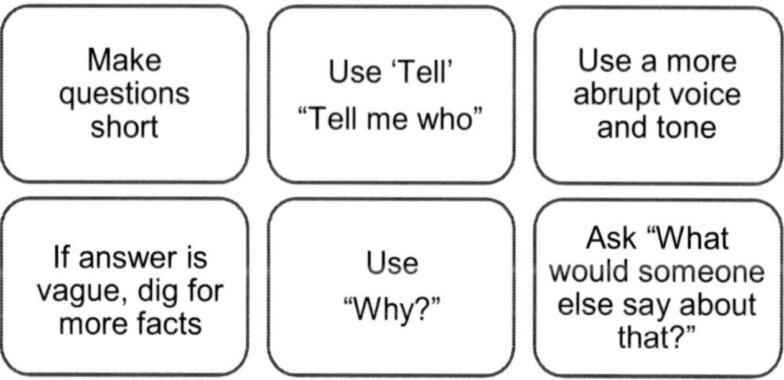

If you are asking supportive questions and feel a more creatively-challenging question will help, you can always signal the change by asking "Would you mind if I ask a more challenging question?"

Chapter review

Reflect on the following questions to challenge yourself and to decide what you will do differently knowing all you have learned from reading this chapter.

Be agile in your support and challenge

- How perfect is the balance of your support and challenge for your staff members?
- Which of your staff would benefit from more support from you?
- Which of your staff would benefit from more constructive challenge from you?
- What will you do to adjust the balance of your support and challenge?

30

Ask questions before giving advice

You don't need to know everything immediately and you probably don't need to know everything to be effective!

As managers and leaders, it's tempting to believe that when someone approaches us for our opinion, we should have the answer immediately to hand. If we don't, we are not doing our job properly.

It's a belief developed by the way we have been trained and educated and often influenced by how past managers have acted towards us.

Our intent may be to quickly help someone by sharing what we know. But in reality, our quickly served advice will be even more helpful if we find out a little more before we answer.

Perhaps you remember an occasion when you started to ask someone for help and received their advice before you had even finished explaining what you wanted the advice for.

How did you feel about them replying that way? Were you impressed at their speed? Frustrated that they didn't invest time really listening to you? Concerned that their advice might not apply to your circumstances? Unimpressed at their air of self-importance? Did their interruption and quick-fire advice encourage you to feel valued and respected?

As a manager, when you are the person being asked for advice, take simple steps so your response is more likely to have a positive rather than a negative effect.

Firstly, make sure you have heard and understood the full situation before providing any answers. If the individual approaches you when you are short of time, it is fine to say "I'm really busy right now and want to make sure I can pay attention. Let's have this conversation at eleven o'clock." When you do get together, listen carefully and hear all they have to say before asking questions to clarify exactly what they do need and want from you. Only then, give advice or answer their questions.

Secondly, no one expects you to be the all-knowing font of all answers. Take inspiration from the 2016 study by Dublin University researchers who devised a test to illustrate how well experts remembered facts. They discovered experts are more likely to make mistakes about their specialist subject because knowing a lot about something doubles the risk of false memories.

It's perfectly acceptable to say "I don't know." or "I can't remember." and then "I'll find out and tell you immediately."

If 'immediately' isn't appropriate, set a date or time and keep to it. This leaves the individual with a sense you are investing time to get them the right answer and provides the opportunity to negotiate the urgency of your response.

Chapter review

Reflect on the following questions to challenge yourself and to decide what you will do differently knowing all you have learned from reading this chapter.

Ask questions before giving advice

- How effective is your balance of questioning vs giving advice?
- In the past, which has been your default response to a question: giving an immediate answer, or asking something?
- What assumptions guide you in deciding whether to ask or to answer? How often do you check those assumptions are still ok?
- What positive impression could you give by asking more questions?

31

Role model what you want them to do

For individuals wanting to develop themselves, it's very helpful for them to observe someone who is successfully modelling the skills and behaviours they want to develop.

As a line manager, you're in a position to help your team member understand which skills and behaviours you need them to develop. You're often also in a position to set an example, or role model, how they should be demonstrated. So, check to ensure you are visibly demonstrating what you are expecting of them.

For example, if you've discussed having greater impact in meetings, and a behaviour such as speaking up positively, then ensure when you are in a meeting together, you encourage them to speak up. Also role model the behaviours yourself. Discuss beforehand how you are planning to do this, and then review afterwards to ensure the two of you have learned from the experience.

The person doing the role modelling does not necessarily have to be their manager. As you reflect on what your staff member needs to develop, decide who could be a useful role model, and could be observed demonstrating the skills, behaviours or approach you wish your staff member to focus on. (See the section Use your network on page 235 for more.)

Chapter review

Use the following questions to reflect and challenge yourself, and to decide what you will do differently knowing all you have learned from reading this chapter.

Role model what you want them to do

- Which behaviours and skills are you aware you are role modelling in a positive way?
- Which of your behaviours and skills would you *not* wish your staff to copy?
    - What will you change?
- Who do you regard as a good role model for skills and behaviours you would like to develop?

32

Have 'adult to adult' conversations

As managers, whether we are having a conversation with staff about good things, or not so good things, we need to show respect by approaching our conversations with an adult-to-adult attitude.

Whenever we interact with another person we adopt an opinion of ourselves, and an opinion of the other person. Transactional Analysis theory describes this as viewing ourselves as either OK or Not OK, and viewing the other person as either OK or Not OK. Combinations of these are represented in the following graphic and describe four different attitudes.

You are OK

I am not OK			I am OK
	I'M NOT OK YOU'RE OK Lose - Win I don't express my opinion I feel insignificant	**I'M OK YOU'RE OK** Win - Win I respect myself & you I feel happy, sad, scared but that's ok	
	I'M NOT OK YOU'RE NOT OK Lose - Lose I don't respect myself I blame others I feel you and I are useless	**I'M OK YOU'RE NOT OK** Win - Lose I need to be in control because I know best I often feel aggressive	

You are not OK

You have the freedom of choice

Harris, Thomas A., 1969

As we approach a development discussion with someone, it can be easy to assume we have knowledge or power which they do not, and that we are there to pass our wisdom to them.

If we do this, we can unconsciously take the position that we're OK and they are not, meaning we know the right answer for them (and they'd better listen to it). We may be tempted to tell them what they should to be doing and how to go about it. In doing so, we're holding a parent position and putting them into the position of the child.

Holding the attitude of I'm OK, You're Not OK can be a stressful position for managers, because it means we need to know what the right answer is for the person and be able to tell them. If they question us or do not agree, we can interpret this as a personal challenge to our authority and respond strongly and negatively.

The implication of this for the other person is they take on the I'm Not OK position and assume we are in the I'm OK position. They will defer to us and accept whatever we tell them to do whether they agree to it or not.

So, when we discuss development plans it's important our staff members do not leave with a plan we have written for them, and an impression that "My manager always knows best." If this happens, there's a risk they will walk away with a plan they know is flawed but will not comment or suggest improvements because in their mind their manager knows something they don't. Potentially, they will walk away knowing they have a plan but have no ownership of delivering it.

If you find a direct report has nodded and agreed in a development planning meeting, but there is no progress with the plan afterwards, this may suggest a 'manager knows best' mindset has affected them. Time for you take action to reset their assumption to I'm OK, You're OK, and renew the discussion.

Choose I'm Ok, You're OK

It's far more constructive to go into a development discussion holding yourself firmly in a position of I'm OK, You're OK. In this state, you know you don't have all of the answers and can remain curious about what the other person wants now and in their future.

You can explore their thinking and make sure they develop their own plan. You can offer your support without feeling concerned if the other person finds their own, better, solution. For them, they have the opportunity to express their view and opinions without the fear of personal judgement. They can develop their own thinking and own the plan and the outcome.

Choosing an 'I'm Ok, You're OK' mind-set is a strong foundation for setting the tone of an adult-to-adult conversation. You cannot control whether the person you are talking to will respond in an equally adult-to-adult style, but that is their choice. Your job is to maintain your professionalism by role-modelling the desired behaviour.

There's more you can do to strengthen the adult-to-adult tone and content of your conversation:

Be careful with your language. When your direct report expresses an idea which you disagree with, it's essential you clearly communicate that it's the idea you don't agree with, not the person. Use a phrase such as "The idea doesn't work for me, what other options are there?" rather than "You're wrong." The right words, focused on the idea, will encourage someone to continue to have ideas and share them. The wrong words could mean they never offer you an idea again.
Rephrasing a sentence by replacing 'you' with 'I' is an established way of getting a point across without sounding confrontational. A key skill when you need your conversations to remain creative. For example, replace "You haven't delivered the report yet" with "I haven't received the report yet."

Choose the environment. Choose the environment and room layout so it is appropriate for your discussion. Neil remembers attending a parent-teacher evening to discuss his son's early-years education. The teacher was sitting on his own adult chair behind a large desk and both Neil and his son were expected to sit on small chairs designed for seven-year-old children. The chair height difference immediately projected a parent-child conversation causing Neil and many other parents to feel uncomfortable, reminded of their own school days. In the workplace, to promote an adult to adult conversation, avoid a location and furniture which places you at a level higher than your staff member.
To create a more positive environment, consider what would work well for the other person as well as yourself. Ask them where they would like to meet. If appropriate, give them the option of deciding exactly when to meet. Find a neutral and

confidential space where you can sit near to each other, sharing the discussion and discussion materials. Sitting on adjacent sides of a table can reinforce a collaborative discussion and avoids signalling an 'opposing sides' discussion which is often associated with sitting on opposite sides of a table.

Decide who holds the pen. The person holding the pen has the power. If you hold the pen and write the notes it's likely they will use your vocabulary and you'll write down what's important to you. Far better to let the other person write the notes. If anything is critically important to you, you can always make sure you ask them to include it. If you need to draw a diagram or write something down, then hand it to them to keep. If your organisation requires a formal record of the discussion let them take the notes and then you can both agree on a summary after the meeting.

Avoid saying "It's difficult." If the conversation you need to have isn't one you are looking forward to, don't tell yourself, or anyone else, you're going to be having a 'difficult conversation.' If you approach the conversation feeling it is going to be difficult, you are more likely to find it is difficult, partly because you will be projecting some emotion which the person you are talking to will react to. Think of it as a 'straight-forward' or 'brutal facts' conversation.

Prepare your adult-to-adult conversation. Decide what you want to communicate and decide your desired outcomes from the conversation. If there's a problem then decide what you feel the problem is, what the other person may feel the problem is and, again, what you want to achieve out of the conversation.

Initiate the conversation early. Even if the conversation you need to have isn't one you are looking forward to yet, take action now to schedule that conversation. Early conversations to make small corrections can mean large corrections don't need to be made at all.

Allowing time to pass before talking to a staff member, while an issue builds and builds in your mind, risks the other person feeling as though they have been ambushed.

Ask for their side of the story. Make time to ask them for their perspective and listen carefully and with interest to what they say. The act of sharing their perspective with you will greatly increase their willingness to reflect on your side of the story. By sharing stories there's a good chance both of you will learn something from the conversation and reach a better understanding.

Keep your conversation focused: During the conversation remember your desired outcomes and maintain your focus on achieving them. Steer away from unhelpful distractions so you'll achieve what you planned.

Each of these tips is easy to use. A little concentration is all you need to set the tone of your conversation as adult-to-adult and to role model an adult-to-adult attitude. It's all about showing respect for the person you are talking to, as a human being.

Chapter review

Use the following reflective questions to challenge yourself, and to decide what you will do differently knowing all that has occurred to you while reading this chapter.

Have 'adult to adult' conversations

- What thoughts and ideas struck you while reading about adult to adult conversations?
- Which conversations do you need to change to a more adult to adult style?
- How could an attitude of 'I'm OK, You're OK' help you and your organisation?
- What clues will help you notice when you have slipped out of an 'I'm OK, You're Ok' attitude?

33

Use your network

We meet many managers who are struggling to do everything themselves, and forget they have wider resources available to them. We all have networks of contacts within our organisations and these can be useful in a number of ways when developing staff.

First of all, we need to recognise we do not know everything, nor do we need to. There will be other people in the organisation who have knowledge or insights into particular areas of development.

So, how can your network help you?

Here are some ideas:

- Mentoring a staff member or yourself
- Coaching a staff member or yourself
- Providing influence to help you obtain what you need
- Describing how a department fits into the broader organisation
- Providing an alternative perspective by using a different learning or communication style
- Providing accurate third party feedback
- Providing a good role model an individual can observe and learn from
- Identifying project opportunities
- Providing knowledge of future roles to you or your report

Many people are happy to support someone who is actively seeking ways in which to develop. They have often been in the same situation themselves. As long as they are not going to have to spend a lot of time working out what is required, many will do their best to support a direct request. After all, they may well want your assistance too.

Chapter review

Use the following reflective questions to challenge yourself, and to decide what you will do differently knowing all that has occurred to you while reading this chapter.

Use your network

To apply the benefits of your network into your own organisational situation:

- Who makes up your network?
- What are their skills, knowledge and experience?
- How could they help you develop your staff?
- What will you personally offer to others when you are part of their network?
- How can doing this help your whole organisation develop?
- How will you engage your network in the development of your staff?

34

Set learning targets

To contribute to an individual reaching their ready-now goal, you can provide a learning targets framework for their development. The framework will develop motivation because it builds on outcome thinking, and because it can set the balance of challenge versus capability at a level which encourages the individual to be in FLOW.

Building the 'content' of a learning targets framework with the individual is essential, but you can start by familiarising yourself with a framework before your conversation. The following figure illustrates a framework which you can use and tailor to suit your needs. We have populated it with an example, shown in italics.

Learning Targets Framework

Learning Targets Framework	
The Big Picture Purpose: *To prepare for working effectively in large teams where I am the only team member with my specialist knowledge*	
My outcome 1	*I have ended each team meeting having made a positive contribution*
Success will look like	*My ideas were welcomed and influential. My questions and advice helped the team understand more and make decisions. I have a good relationship with team members*
My current level of capability	*I wait to be invited to speak. I rely on my manager to make preparations. I only concentrate on agenda items related to my own specialism*
Improvement steps I'll take	*I will prepare my own desired outcomes for each meeting, and contribute to the agenda. I'll take steps so I am prepared to achieve the outcomes*
When	*Preparations 1 week before each meeting & action during each meeting*
Review of my progress	*(to be added at progress review in 2 months)*
My outcome 2	

Understanding the framework

The following section describes how each component of the framework is used.

The 'big picture purpose' prompt is a reminder to capture what all the development targets are aiming towards. Refer to this regularly as you discuss and develop the content of the framework, and also as you regularly review progress against the targets. Repeated reminders of the purpose help to provide context for the targets. This guides the way the targets are approached giving a sense of direction rather than in isolation.

Framework - My Outcomes: These are described briefly in the past tense as if they have been successfully completed and describe what needs to have been achieved rather than what steps needed to be taken to achieve it.

For example, an outcome of 'I have ended each team meeting having made a positive contribution' is stated in the past tense and describes the what will have happened, not all the steps needed to make it happen.

Outcomes must be described with accuracy and clarity, and are a more powerful measure than checking what steps have been completed. The risk of using only a list of steps is that eventually all the steps may be completed, but this doesn't necessarily mean the outcome has been achieved.

An example of this risk becoming real was demonstrated by a leadership team whose meeting we regularly facilitated. The group decided to re-write the organisation's job descriptions more accurately and they started to create a tick-list of steps:

- ✓ Decide a template
- ✓ Get draft descriptions written
- ✓ Check descriptions with team leaders
- ✓ Get the descriptions agreed by Human Resources

Because they decided to complete their tick list outside the meeting, they were asked to write down the desired outcome of the initiative. They wrote:

"All staff have received a new role description which is consistent in format to other role descriptions, and matches what is actually done by the person in the job."

When they met to review the initiative two months later they were proud of the progress they had made on the job descriptions. They believed the activity was completed and the team could now move on to develop another goal to achieve. They revealed their tick list, admirably full of ticks, and were asked "As a final check, please read your original desired outcome again and describe how complete it is."

There was a collective sigh and someone breathed "We've finished this one." Then a voice spoke out. "Reading through this, we've accomplished a lot of agreement and consultation about the job descriptions in an amazingly short time, but our desired outcome says 'our staff' have a new role description. So far, I know 'we' all have a copy of these descriptions but who has sent them out to our staff?" There was an awkward silence as they realised that while they had completed the list of valuable, essential tasks, it did not add up to achieving their desired outcome.

Outcomes can also be valuable for reducing the number of steps which need to be taken.

If we keep in mind what the outcome is, then it's possible we may only complete half of the steps planned, but notice our objective is achieved. We can stop and direct our energy towards a new goal.

As an example of this, when Katya was planning a performance review meeting for one of her staff, her desired outcome was that she and her team member would begin the meeting well prepared.

Her list of steps to achieve this were:

- ✓ Find the performance review guide and make own performance notes
- ✓ Ask the team member to make their own preparatory notes
- ✓ Ask the team member to bring feedback from their key customers with them
- ✓ Remind the team member again, a few days before the meeting, to bring notes and feedback

She found the guide and made her own notes for the meeting, and then unexpectedly received an email from the staff member. He'd proactively sent her a copy of his performance notes and the feedback he'd collected from his customers. Katya hadn't personally completed all the steps in her plan, but decided the good preparations outcome was complete.

Framework - Success will look like: In the Learning Targets Framework add an example or two of what success will be like when the outcome has been achieved. Good inspiration for the examples of success can come from asking "When you are successful in achieving this outcome, what will you see, hear, feel, say?"

Framework - **My Current Level Of Capability:** Compare the Examples of Success with the current situation and capability. Make a note of the current level of capability so the framework supports a view of current reality plus the goal. The notes describing current capability form the starting point for noticing progress during the regular review sessions.

Framework - Improvement steps I'll take: Jointly develop several significant steps which will contribute to achieving the outcome. They can be steps to get things started, or steps which describe milestones along the road to achieving the outcome. Remember, achieving the outcome is the goal so, over time, the steps may change, or they may reduce or increase in number. Completion is measured by whether the outcome has been achieved, not by completion of the steps. It may be appropriate to support or even congratulate your team member when they cancel or change steps because they are no longer required.

Framework - When: Make a note of approximately when a step should be completed. As a minimum this information encourages a discussion about resources and timing, competing priorities and overall duration of the personal development activities.

Framework - Review Of My Progress. During regular reviews of the individual's progress, this part of the framework catalyses discussion about the overall change which has occurred, and the change since the last review. During the review, ensure you positively recognise progress made and discuss what your team member has learned from both what occurred as planned, and what did not.

Use Their Preferred Learning Styles

Your discussions to develop the learning targets will involve you asking for suggestions from your team members and giving them helpful options or possible solutions. Remember: when you offer them options and solutions they are not you! They will have their own preferences for how they like to learn, how they think, even how they like to be recognised for good work. If you enjoy learning best by reading lots of books before you start something, you might have assumed the pre-reading route is the best way to learning for everyone. That isn't the case, and we will each learn more effectively if our personal, preferred learning style is taken into account. The section Fine-tuning how you learn, to learn more effectively on page 73, describes in more depth these learning style differences and how to use them.

Chapter review

Use the following reflective questions to challenge yourself, and to decide what you will do differently knowing all that has occurred to you while reading this chapter.

Set learning targets

- How well do your staff understand their learning targets?
    - How do you know?
- How often are their learning targets described as outcomes instead of tick-list tasks?
- What's one thing you will change to support their targeted learning?

35

Coach as well as mentor

In competitive sports, the trainer gives the sportsperson advice and instructions to improve their performance. Often the trainer will have reached an advanced level of the sport themselves so they can say "I know what I'm talking about" and "I speak from personal experience." Gradually the performance level of the sportsperson will rise and rise, as they benefit from this advice. But what happens when the sportsperson reaches the level equal to that of their trainer? How can the trainer talk from experience to guide the sportsperson to achieve an even higher level?

An obvious solution is to hire a more accomplished trainer who has personally reached an even higher performance level. But how does that work if we want the sportsperson to break a world record? No one has ever been at such a high level of performance before so it's going to be impossible to find someone who can help the sportsperson by telling them how they did it. This is where the coaching approach comes in.

Back in the workplace, you want to support the development of staff members, and you can do some of the development by sharing your experiences and giving advice. This is a mentoring approach.

The challenge comes when the development a staff member needs goes beyond the level of skill, knowledge or experience you personally possess. Does this mean, like the sports trainer, you must be placed on the bench, waiting for someone new who we *can* help with our advice? No. Not at all.

The solution is to switch to using a coaching approach instead of a mentoring approach. Once you learn how to switch, you'll have the capability to support the development of someone up to and beyond your own level of skills, knowledge and experience. You can even support someone who needs to develop skills in a discipline you know little or nothing about.

When you use more coaching, you'll find the staff you coach need to come to you for less and less help, because coaching increases their capability to solve their own problems. They'll only come to you with the significant stuff. Let's look a little further into coaching and mentoring to understand why.

"The significant problems we face cannot be solved at the same level of thinking we were at when we created them."
Albert Einstein

Coaching compared to mentoring

There are significant differences between the approach used to coach someone and the approach used to mentor. Both have their benefits, time and place. As a reminder, the following illustrates the key differences and benefits.

The coaching style

- Asks questions
- Focuses on goals or outcomes
- Focuses on the coachee
- Coach chosen independent of skills and knowledge
- Coachee owns the outcomes

The mentoring style

- Tells, gives opinions, provides answers
- Focuses on skills or experience
- Focus is often on the mentor
- Mentor chosen because of their skills and knowledge
- Mentor follows up on delivery

Have a mentoring conversation when ...

- Someone needs a quick start
- You need to boost someone's knowledge about a subject
- You want to set expectations
- Advice from you will be influential in influencing others

Have a coaching conversation when ...

- You want to help someone clarify their thinking and increase their confidence in what they know
- You want to encourage different solutions or novel thinking
- You want to explore options
- You need to know more about an opportunity or problem

There are coaches who include some mentoring-advice into their conversations, and there are mentors who will include coaching-style questions in their conversations. But, for the purposes of this book, when we refer to coaching and mentoring we will be applying the descriptions above.

I understand the difference; how does that help me?

Mentoring is a skill most of us have experienced at some point because it forms part of what every teacher does. A teacher tells us information. A teacher responds to our questions with an answer. A teacher shows us when we have gone wrong and corrects us.

As a manager, you will often be expected to act in a similar way. Your staff want to know what to do. So you tell them. They want to hear you explain how to do something, so you tell them. Taken to an extreme, you may sometimes have felt you were expected to know 'all' the answers.

When we need to develop a team member we have a choice; mentor them and tell them what they need to know, or coach them, helping them learn for themselves, helping them appreciate they know more than they realise.

The following illustrate when coaching is valuable to use and when not to use it.

X Don't use a coaching style

Basic info	When someone starts in a job and needs basic information
Set goals	When setting goals or expectations for staff
Answers	When the individual is expecting to be told the answer
Emergency	When rules need to be explained or emergency instructions given
Other help	When the help needed is mentoring, counselling, or another service

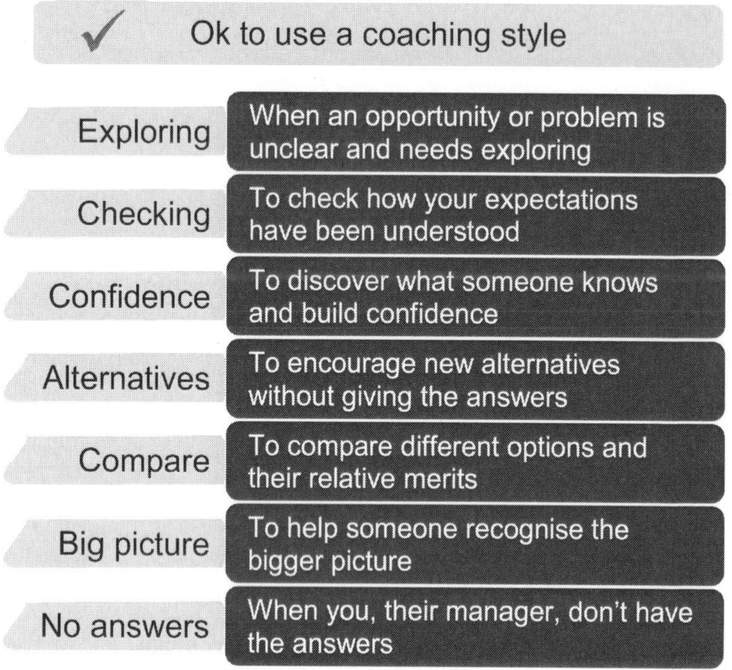

Ok to use a coaching style
Exploring
When an opportunity or problem is unclear and needs exploring
Checking
To check how your expectations have been understood
Confidence
To discover what someone knows and build confidence
Alternatives
To encourage new alternatives without giving the answers
Compare
To compare different options and their relative merits
Big picture
To help someone recognise the bigger picture
No answers
When you, their manager, don't have the answers

If you habitually use only the mentoring approach you can suppress the development of your staff and reduce their level of engagement in their work. They can feel as if they're not allowed to generate new ideas or alternative ways of doing things, and that their opinions aren't valued. You may be inadvertently creating the view "There's only one way and it's the boss's way."

Using coaching questions, you'll draw out what the other person currently knows, and what they don't know. You'll encourage them to have new ideas and, because a coaching approach is not judgemental, you can ask questions to inspire them to analyse their own ideas for suitability, and choose the best.

A coaching approach, used in the appropriate context, will bring these benefits and more to the person you are coaching and, significantly, it will bring a host of benefits to your organisation. A study by Manchester Consulting Inc. in 2001, chose the goal of determining the impact of coaching on the organisation. The results showed that 53% of the organisations gained an increase in productivity, almost the same number noticed an increase in the quality of the output, 77% found an improvement in relationships between managers and their staff, and a third were already noticing a positive effect on staff retention.

If you need further convincing that a coaching question style is a powerful technique, apply it in situations when you want to contribute, but have little or no knowledge of the subject. Perhaps the situation will be supporting a staff member in exploring a role you know nothing about. Or participating in a management team discussion, on a subject which is outside your expertise. The opportunities are numerous, and you can make a valuable contribution with little or no specialist knowledge.

As an example, Fiona was invited to bring her coaching skills to a meeting. The objective of the meeting was for a group of senior leaders to listen to the progress of several projects and decide whether the projects should continue, be given more money, or be stopped.

Fiona had no experience of the projects' content and had never been part of a project review panel before.

After the first, nervous, project leader had presented his project update, one leader asked:

"So, the project is 6 months behind target?"

"Yes." replied the project manager.

"And you don't think you can catch up?" Questioned another leader.

"That's correct."

"And 6 month's delay means you would deliver the results too late for the other teams to benefit from them?"

"Yes. We're sure the other teams could make valuable decisions, using our results. Decisions which could boost profits, but their decisions will have been taken before we finish now."

"Before we pass judgement on you project, let's ask our new coach if she can contribute anything here."

Fiona hadn't any experience of the specialist technology being discussed, but she could ask general coaching-style questions.

"What is the most important contributor to the speed of your project now?" prompted Fiona.

"It's all about people power at this point. The work can be divided into lots of pieces but we only have a limited number of people in the project team."

"How many people would you need in the team now, to get your project finished on time or earlier?"

"Another two people for three months would bring the project in on time."

"Who could help you get those extra people for that time?"

"Well, I had hoped this review panel could help me."

"Ok, so what would you like to ask them then?"

"OK. Now you've all heard the project update, and about the delay. Would you be prepared to give us two more team members for three months so the other teams can get our results in time to improve their decisions?"

The leaders looked at each other and nodded. The chair responded "Yes, of course. That's what these meetings are for. We'll arrange what you need immediately. This sounds like a very promising project!"

Fiona's coaching style used 'common sense' open questions which uncovered more information and turned the conversation into a much more creative one. She made a truly valuable difference to the conversation, without having any specialist knowledge.

Remember to use open questions to discover more. Target your questions so they move the conversation and situation forward. Even when the conversation is about a less desirable situation, or something which hasn't worked, you can still make your questions creative and forward looking by asking "What have you learned?" and "How will you apply this learning to improve future opportunities?"

To find out your default coaching or mentoring style use the questions in the appendix Am I Coaching or a Mentoring Manager? Questionnaire on page 309.

Chapter review

Use the following reflective questions to challenge yourself, and to decide what you will do differently knowing all that has occurred to you while reading this chapter.

Coach as well as mentor

- Which is your dominant style: coaching or mentoring?
- In which of your situations could a change of style possibly bring more success?
- How do you decide which style you will use?
- What could remind you to make that choice a more active one?
- How do you explain or share which style you will use?
- What will you do differently in your balance of coaching and mentoring now?

36

Get feedback for your staff and feedback from your staff

To support your staff member to become ready-now, you can make a substantial contribution by:

- asking stakeholders for feedback about your staff member
- asking your staff member for feedback about how well you are supporting them

Asking stakeholders for feedback

By asking for this feedback you're raising the visibility of your direct report; attracting the attention of the stakeholder to the individual, and to what the individual is contributing. By asking carefully worded open questions when you ask for feedback you can gently encourage the feedback to focus on the strengths and gaps of the individual.

As busy humans, we can shorten conversations by saying "no." when we're asked for something. When you ask for feedback ask in a way which can't be answered with a 'no'. For example, to ask for feedback about visibility, replace "Are you seeing anything of Jenny's work?" with "How much are you seeing of Jenny's work?" This can't be answered with yes or no so you are more likely to learn more from the answer.

Set a positive tone in your questions when asking about gaps, and make them specific. Replace "Has Johan stopped having issues with presentations?" with "How much has Johan's presentation content improved?"

Add your desired outcome into the question to set the direction you want to achieve.

Replace "Is Johan still struggling?" with "What changes are you seeing which show Johan is closer to being ready for a new role?" You may hear a very positive answer or you may hear the reasons why Johan is no nearer to being ready. Either way, you'll receive information which will be helpful to your support of the staff member.

When you receive their feedback, pass it on constructively to your staff member. Talk to them honestly about the feedback. Be precise and check their understanding. Ask them what the implications of the feedback might be, how the implications contribute to the plan to become ready-now, and what new steps are needed.

When you ask for feedback from stakeholders, remember you are modelling good leadership behaviours. By asking for feedback, you are demonstrating that you have the interests and development of your staff in your hands. This may well encourage a reciprocal request for feedback about staff in a different group. It also provides an opportunity to share, even briefly, ideas for how improvements can be made.

When a stakeholder feels they have had a light, constructive role in the development of a staff member, it can encourage them to more strongly support that staff member achieving their goals.

Asking staff members for feedback

Finally, ask your staff member for feedback about how well you are supporting them.

During the time your staff member is working on their plan to fill the gaps, ask them regularly to reflect on what and how you are contributing. A helpful question to ask is "What could I do differently so my support becomes more helpful to you?"

Chapter review

Use the following reflective questions to challenge yourself, and to decide what you will do differently knowing all that has occurred to you while reading this chapter.

Get feedback for your staff and feedback from your staff

- How often do you ask stakeholders for their feedback about individual members of your staff?
- What could be the benefit from asking a little more often?
- How do you currently ask staff members for feedback about how well you are supporting them?
- What could you do to make their feedback even more valuable to you?

37

Provide 'breathing space'

Once you've identified what your report needs to do to develop for their next role, remember a key resource they'll need is time. They may need time for study, visiting other departments, shadowing others or to practise their new skills. Make this time an explicit part of your resource planning discussions and tell your staff members that you expect them to spend time on their development, either to become expert at their existing roles, or to become prepared for their next role.

We meet managers who say "but I haven't got enough resources to deliver what I need to now, never mind giving someone time for their development." In our experience, by allowing people time to develop, you gain time as they become more motivated, more efficient and discover new ways to do things. While there may be an initial cost, there is a big payback available. You'll also notice that, when someone is aware of an active investment in their development, the organisation gains because they work harder. You might also obtain helpful, extra resources by offering opportunities for others to come and gain experience alongside your staff.

Chapter review

Use the following reflective questions to challenge yourself, and to decide what you will do differently knowing all that has occurred to you while reading this chapter.

Provide 'breathing space'

- How much breathing space do your staff need so they have the opportunity to develop?
- What do you need to do to create breathing space?
- What is the consequence of you *not* providing that breathing space?

38

This isn't just about your staff! What about you?

By adopting the approaches in the How to help a staff member become ready-now chapters you'll already have strengthened yourself as a good leader and manager. As you embark on these steps, and develop them to suit your environment and style, remember that they can inform you of what to expect from your own manager.

You should be having your own development discussions, taking the initiative yourself. Use the first chapters in this book to prompt your thinking about your direction and give your manager and stakeholders information which will allow them to help you achieve your goals. If they need ideas for how to help you can lend them this book or, even better, buy them a copy of their own!

39

Succession Planning

You may have recognised the approach of encouraging someone from being ready-later to ready-now is a key component of succession planning. Succession planning is a powerful contributor to ensuring the success of an organisation now and in the future. Sometimes overlooked in favour of concentrating solely on hiring and training staff into a single job, succession planning is about managing the skills, knowledge and experience within an organisation over time, so the organisation's targets and goals can be achieved.

The most talked about and written about succession planning examples tend to be focused on the most senior roles in an organisation, but succession planning is worth discussing for all levels of staff in an organisation.

The purpose of succession planning (& the risks of not doing it)

Succession planning has a clue to its purpose in the name; 'success'.

Succession Planning makes sure there is, or will be, a good match between the human skills and behaviours *needed* to generate success for the organisation, and the *actual* humans and skills available.

Not having any level of succession planning in your organisation risks your business performance dropping below the expected level. This can be caused by a sudden loss of senior C-Level (e.g. CIO, CFO) skills, a sudden loss of hard-to-come-by entry level skills or a loss of skill levels between the two. The drop-in business performance may hit the bottom-line of profits directly, or it may do so by causing reputational damage.

The good news is a little succession planning, integrated into your regular people development processes, can decrease the occurrence of these skill losses and significantly improve how fast you can respond if the unexpected does occur.

By engaging in some level of succession planning you can pull in additional valuable benefits too.

- You can develop candidates so that when an existing staff member moves out of a role, there's someone available in the wings to replace them, and the business can continue to run in a stable way

- You can support your staff in achieving their career goals by having a succession plan to illustrate their path from their current role to their career goal, highlighting which strengths and gaps are relevant to their future

- You can tailor and focus staff training and development plans so the skills, knowledge, experience and behaviours which are needed in the organisation's roles are available in the right people at the right time. If you discover internal candidates will not be available in time for a role, you can plan ahead and identify routes for bringing in external resources at the right time

Use the content of a succession plan to help identify when external drivers are changing what is needed in future roles. For example, if external conditions drive the need to outsource, then new types of collaborative and negotiation skills will be needed.
The four core steps of succession planning are:

1) **Identify key roles and the skills, knowledge and experience they demand.** When you're clear what competencies a role needs, check if the needs can be easily met with readily available staff. If so, then no extra planning may be needed other than recognising the delays caused by recruitment lead times (to replace someone leaving) and being prepared to make recruiting decisions in a timely way. Add a regular check to monitor whether any internal or external changes have made a difference to the supply of, and demand for, key competencies. If the competencies for some roles are in short supply, then the following steps are needed for those roles.

2) **Create succession approaches.** For each of the roles which need succession planning attention, decide an approach to ensure the competencies will be available despite any movement of individual staff members.
   The approach can include creating personal development paths for internal staff, identifying external temporary sources of the competencies, recruiting new sources, and creating retention arrangements which reduce the occurrences of sudden, unexpected competency shortages.

3) **Communicate the succession approaches and make them happen.** Succession plans and approaches are far more successful when they are specific, precise, written down and communicated well. Link succession approaches into regular development planning and performance reviews so they are part of everyday processes.

4) **Review how successful the succession approaches are, and what has changed.** Annually review the competency supply and demand, noticing where new competencies are required, where good progress is being made on maintaining competencies, and optimising your approach to further raise your succession plan effectiveness.

Remember, however detailed or light your succession planning is, having the succession discussions with your peers, senior stakeholders and staff makes a positive difference, and you may be surprised at the new opportunities which will emerge for your staff while you are ensuring the success of your organisation.

Chapter review

Use the following questions to reflect on what you have learned and decide what you will now do differently knowing all that has occurred to you while reading this chapter.

Succession planning

- How strong is your succession planning for your organisation?
- What advantages could emerge from making it stronger?
- What will you do differently in your succession planning?
- How could succession planning help you in your own progression?

40

Conclusion

Thank you for reading this book and investing in yourself. We are delighted you have taken the time.

In our increasingly competitive world, finding a competitive advantage, like these tools and techniques, can make a real difference to your success in work and life.

The experiences, stories and tools which were new to you in these chapters may have looked like common sense and easy-to-learn as you read them.

Good. They are.

Your competitive advantage and new success for yourself and those around you, will come from simply turning this common sense into common practice.

You can do this, often with minimal or no extra effort, by following the stages we've described.

You will already have had new ideas about what is next for you, and feelings of excitement and motivation which come from the confidence of having the tools to achieve what you need to do.

Now is the time to turn thought into action.

Set your direction. Set positive expectations for yourself. Use the steps we have described. Remember to couple the power of being persistent to achieve what you want, with flexibility in the route you choose to get there.

Challenge yourself and be kind to yourself as you take action and move from ready-later to ready-now!

41

A letter from the authors and their offer to you

Dear Reader.

We hope you enjoyed reading *Moving From Ready Later To Ready Now.*

Thank you for getting hold of a copy!

While we were writing this book, we received lots of ideas from colleagues and clients, friends and family. They shared stories about the tools they found most helpful, and about their renewed enthusiasm to pass their learning on to others.

We enjoy receiving ideas and feedback to help us in our drive to share what we've learned and make a difference.

So, drop us a line and tell us what was new to you, which sections you liked most, and even those you liked the least and how we can improve them. You can write to us at:

DaveNeilRL2RN@ccmrconsulting.com

We've also heard from readers who've told us their stories of how these skills and approaches have helped them, their families, communities and work colleagues. We're always excited to hear these stories: they help us share our learning in new ways and open our minds to the huge number of opportunities there are to benefit from using these skills.

Thanks again to all those who've shared their stories already!

We'd like to hear about *your* stories too; your successes, what you've learned, and the tips you'd like to share.

Of course, we all learn from things which did not go as we intended, so share those with us. Join us in developing a mind set of "There's no such thing as failure, only feedback to help us decide what we do next!"

Please send your stories and tips to:

DaveNeilRL2RN@ccmrconsulting.com

We'd love to be able to add some of them to our next edition or include them in one of our tip-sheets.

Our readers often want to know where they can learn more and when our next publication or workshop will occur, so we've added a section after this letter to give you the scoop.

Thank you again for reading *Moving From Ready Later To Ready Now* and for sharing your time with us.

Wishing you success.

David Smith and Neil Raval

42

How to learn more

Learning More: Templates and advice for you and your team

As well as being valuable to you as an individual, a team member or a manager, the approaches in this book have proven to be a firm foundation for building high performing teams in a wide variety organisation and at all levels.

If you'd like an easy way of obtaining a printable copy of the templates from the book, so you can write on them or share them with a team, download a copy from: ccmrconsulting.com/books. Look for them on the resources tab.

We'll be happy to give advice on using the worksheets so drop us a line to **DaveNeilRL2RN@ccmrconsulting.com** if you are wondering how best to incorporate them when you are planning for positive change, creating credible personal development plans, effectively engaging influencers, and more.

Learning More: Building relationships, influencing and getting your point heard

Our section Building rapport using awareness of communication styles, on page 90, describes how you can increase your influence substantially by simply having an understanding of how you communicate, how others may be different and what you can do about it. As we work with clients across the world, many tell us they would like to learn more about how to use the influence of different communication styles effectively, starting by understanding their own preferences.

To fill this gap for yourself, and gain an advantage which many others do not yet have, contact us for our communications styles questionnaire and personal, verbal feedback. The insightful, practical feedback will apply what you learn directly to your own real world situations to help you the most.

To get the advantages of understanding and using different communications styles for yourself, contact us at: **comstyles@ccmrconsulting.com**.
We'll explain what to do and the simple step to get access to this service for you, or for you and your team.

Learning More: Our Tips At Your Finger Tips

From our experience, we know you'll begin to notice more and more opportunities to use the approaches in this book to bring positive results for yourself and those around you. Like you, our other readers and class members enjoy how easily they learn these skills. They've asked how they can get occasional reminders of how to use a tool, or how to word a question so their skills always feel ready-to-go.

To help, we're developing a phone app designed specially as an aid to keeping these skills alive and kicking. You'll be able to add it to your smart phone and use it to remind yourself about the approaches and tools. You'll find short hints and tips to help you in the moment and you'll find a link to our website so you can keep an eye out for how to learn more at one of our workshops.

Check for availability of the phone app on the resources page of ccmrconsulting.com/books. Better still, drop us a line at **DaveNeilRL2RN@ccmrconsulting.com** to let us know your interest and to find out how the app is progressing.

Acknowledgements

This is the opportunity for us to thank all those who've helped in some way to publish this book.

Yinka, thank you for the challenge which led to the creation of the book. Thanks to the hundreds of members of our CCMR iCoach community, and all those we have coached. You have inspired us to continually improve our skills and programmes and your questions, suggestions and stories make us smile and keep us energised.

Naomi, thank you for your editing skills and patience in working with us. Angela and Paul, thank you for your valuable proof reading. To all our families and friends, thank you for listening as we explored our thinking and for encouraging us both with writing the book and in establishing and developing CCMR

Consulting. Thanks to former managers, and those we have managed and worked with. Your training, insights and experiences have informed our writing.

Finally, to our canine companions, thank you for the company and slightly reproachful glances as we spent time working on the book, rather than walking with you over hills and dales.

Dave and Neil.

References

FLOW : Csikszentmihályi, Mihaly; Flow: The Psychology of Optimal Experience; Harper & Row. Reprinted 2008.

Asking for help: Flynn, Francis, Lake, Vanessa; "If You Need Help, Just Ask": Underestimating Compliance With Direct Requests For Help; Journal of Personality and Social Psychology; 2008. Vol. 95, Issue 1, Pages 128-143.

Soft Skills: Medland, Dina;, Quantifying The Value Of 'Soft Skills'; Forbes.com, March 2015. Research report available at backingsoftskills.co.uk. Accessed March 2016.

Learning Styles Preference: Honey, Peter; The Learning Styles Questionnaire; Honey and Mumford Press. 2006.

Coaching impact on the organisation: McGovern, J, et al., Maximising The Impact Of Executive Coaching, The Manchester Review, 2001; Volume 6, Number 1.

Communication Styles: Merrill, David W. and Reid, Roger H.; Personal Styles & Effective Performance; Chilton Book Co.

Open Questions: http://changingminds.org/techniques/questioning/open_closed_questions.htm; accessed March 2016.

Be More Visible: Lowther, Dianne; Understanding NLP Convincers. From Success Now issue 10, March 1999.

Power up your feedback giving: Brim, B., Asplund, J.; Driving Engagement By Focusing On Strengths; Gallup Business Journal, 2009; Accessed November 2016.

Support & Challenge When Coaching: Blakey, John. and Day, Ian; Challenging Coaching - Going Beyond Traditional Coaching to Face the Facts; Nicholas Brealey Publishing, 2012.

Adult-To-Adult Conversations: Harris, Thomas A.; I'm OK, You're OK; Harper & Row 1969.

Ask questions before giving advice: Deasy, Jamie, Knowing Too Much: Experts More Likely To Experience 'False Memories' About Their Specialist Subject; University College Dublin News, August 2016; Accessed December 2016.

Examples of Personal and Corporate Core Values used in the quiz: http://examples.yourdictionary.com/examples-of-core-values.html; accessed February 2016.

Have Persistence: Campbell, J. P., McColy, R. A., Oppler, S. H., & Sager, C. E.; A Theory of Performance, (1993).

JK Rowling Quote: JK Rowling Harvard Commencement Speech Part 1 - June 5 2008. YouTube

Bibliography

?What If!; Sticky Wisdom; Capstone; 2002

Abraham, Jay; Getting Everything You Can Out Of All You've Got; Piatkus; 2009

Borg, James; Persuasion; Pearson; 2nd Edition 2007

Buckingham, Marcus and Clifton, Donald O.; Now, Discover Your Strength; Simon & Schuster; 2002

Clutterbuck, David; Coaching The Team At Work; Nicholas Brealey; 3rd Edition 2011

Duhigg, Charles; The Power Of Habit; Random House; 2013

Gladwell, Malcolm; The Tipping Point; Abacus; 2000

Godin, Seth; Linchpin; Piatkus; 2010

Pink, Daniel; A Whole New Mind; Marshall Cavendish, 2010

Schein, Edgar; Organisational Culture And Leadership; Jossey-Bass; 3rd Edition 2004

Senge, Peter M.; The Fifth Discipline; Random House; 2006 Edition

Smith, Julien and Brogan, Chris; Trust Agents; Wiley; 2010

Van Rooy, David L,; Trajectory; AMA; 2014

Appendices

In our appendices, you'll find the templates referred to in the book, designed to help you reflect, capture your thinking and plan for the future. Many of them can be downloaded and printed from our website.

Explore the resources section of **www.ccmrconsulting.com/books** to reach them.

Appendix 1

Fitting Work And Life Together

For each component of your life, make a note of your situation now, then the situation you'd like and what you will do to take a step towards reaching it.

	My situation now	The situation I'd like & what I'll do about it
Money		
Work & career		
Play & Leisure		
Relationships		
Spiritual Well-being		
Lifestyle & Possessions		
Health		
Creativity		

Appendix 2

Core Values Quiz

Take this short quiz to identify your core values.

Step 1: Read the list of values below.

Authenticity	Faith	Openness
Achievement	Fame	Optimism
Adventure	Friendships	Peace
Ambition	Fun	Pleasure
Authority	Growth	Popularity
Autonomy	Happiness	Recognition
Boldness	Harmony	Reputation
Compassion	Honesty	Respect
Challenge	Influence	Responsibility
Citizenship	Inner- Harmony	Reward
Community	Integrity	Security
Competency	Justice	Self-Respect
Contribution	Kindness	Service to others
Creativity	Knowledge	Spirituality
Curiosity	Leadership	Stability
Determination	Learning	Success
Diversity	Life-Balance	Status
Efficiency	Love	Trustworthiness
Ethical	Loyalty	Wealth
Fairness	Making A Difference	Wisdom

Step 2: Place the value words into three of your own groups.

(Decide if copying the list, cutting out the words and moving them into groups will work for you)

- Group 1: These values are very important to me
- Group 2: These values have some importance to me
- Group 3: These values have least importance to me

Step 3: Apply a limit of six values in the 'very important' group to drive out which values are most important to you, and what you can do without.

Look for a job which allows you to demonstrate your most important core values. Living your core values will be a strong motivator for you.

Take a look at the 'least important' values group. Decide which of these are actually de-motivators for you. Take action to increase the number of motivating values in your job, and reduce the number of de-motivating values.

http://examples.yourdictionary.com/examples-of-core-values.html

Appendix 3

Template For Self-Assessment Of Strengths And Gaps

Examine each of the skills on the following pages, and assess your own score. The scoring key is:

1 I don't do this yet

2 I'm able to do this with some help

3 I'm competent, without help

4 I'm competent and I'm able to help others to do it

Template for Self-Assessment of Strengths and Gaps

Skill	My Score			
How I solve problems	1	2	3	4
I ask questions to draw out the whole picture of a problem and its implications				
I find out what purpose will be achieved by solving the problem				
I develop several options				
I decide, in a timely way, which solution to use				
I create a plan to implement the solution and share it with others				
I use the plan to deliver the solution				
I monitor the delivery and adapt solutions so the outcome is fit for purpose				

Template for Self-Analysis of Strengths and Gaps (continued)

Skill	My Score			
How I communicate	1	2	3	4
I am competent and confident in presenting oral and visual information				
I flex my language to match the activity e.g. presentations, reports, meetings				
I listen actively and effectively				
I offer constructive criticism				
I use visuals, e.g. charts & diagrams to support verbal and written communication				
I keep to the point				
I match my communication content and style to my audience				

Template for Self-Analysis of Strengths and Gaps (continued)

Skill **How I manage myself**	My Score 1	2	3	4
I manage my time effectively. I meet deadlines and get to meetings on time				
I set realistic objectives, priorities and standards for myself				
I monitor my performance and adapt to increase my performance				
I show flexibility. I'm willing to see there may be more than one way to solve a problem				
I take responsibility for acting in a professional and ethical manner				
I actively ask for feedback, with enough precision to help me learn				
I handle criticism constructively				

Template for Self-Analysis of Strengths and Gaps (continued)

Skill	My Score			
How I manage my learning	1	2	3	4
I take responsibility for my own learning and personal growth				
I understand the learning cycle and ensure I complete the cycle when I'm learning				
I explore different ways of learning				
I regularly reflect on my learning and check it is supporting my progress				
I share my learning with others				
I don't make the same mistake twice				

Template for Self-Analysis of Strengths and Gaps (continued)

Skill **How I work with others**	My Score 1	2	3	4
I respect the views and values of others				
I assist and support others in their learning				
I ensure I have clear goals, take responsibility for them, and deliver				
I adapt to the needs of a group: taking initiative, leading, delegating				
I negotiate effectively with individuals & groups and achieve a win-win outcome				
I work to collective goals: working to agreed plans, within agreed resources				
I monitor processes used by a group working together, and propose improvements				

Template for Self-Assessment of Strengths and Gaps

Skill	My Score 1 2 3 4
My technical and specialised skills	
List your technical and specialised skills below	
Skill 1	☐☐☐☐
Skill 2	☐☐☐☐
Skill 2	☐☐☐☐
Skill 4	☐☐☐☐
Skill 5	☐☐☐☐
Skill 6	☐☐☐☐

Appendix 4

Your Personal Change Planning Template

Use the prompts in each section of the template to stimulate your thinking.

Following the plan template you will find questions to encourage precision into your plan. Read the questions yourself or, even better, get someone else to ask them. You will often find your answer is a little different when someone else is listening.

1. Describe your next role and which skills, knowledge, experience & behaviours are important for being ready for the role. Check out your assumptions so you know you are setting the right goals:

2. Write down which of the necessary skills, knowledge, experience & behaviours you already have at the right level and which you need to maintain:

3. Write down where you currently have gaps in the necessary level of skills, knowledge, experience & behaviours needed to be ready-now for the new role:

4a. Write a list of what you will begin to do, and continue to do, so you demonstrate you are ready-now for the new role.

4b. Write a list of the things you will stop doing or do less of to demonstrate you are ready-now for the new role.

5. Write a list of stages you will use to organise the changes you need to make into manageable pieces: Note several outcomes for each stage and add a desired completion date next to each to give you a timeline to work to. Note next to each outcome who can help or contribute.

6. Now that you have the stages described, write down what you will actually do as your **first step** and when you will do it.

7. Describe how you will monitor and measure your progress.

Appendix 5

Questions To Use With Your Personal Change Planning Template

When you have answered the questions in each part of the personal change planning template, you can stick with what you have written, or you can show an even higher level of motivation by answering the challenging questions below. Each set of questions links to the section of the planning template with the same number.

To start with, choose questions which feel most relevant or significant to you. They will test your thinking and broaden your understanding. To learn more, choose several which seem less directly relevant and discover what new thinking they spark. You'll have noticed earlier in the book we encourage you to talk to other people, sharing your goals and plans and finding out how they can help. You'll learn even more when you are listening to someone else asking you these questions and paying attention to your answers.

Questions

1 Knowing about your target role

- Which skills, knowledge, experience & behaviours are most important to have on day-1 of your target role? For what reasons?
- Who can help you check your assumptions?
- Which of the necessary skills, knowledge, experience & behaviours interest you most?

2 Knowing your strengths

- What is your best source of guidance for deciding the right level of skills, knowledge, experience & behaviours you will need?
- How does using the right skills, knowledge, experience & behaviours at the right level fit with your personal values?
- How will you check you are continuing to operate your strengths at the right level for the new role?

3 Identifying the gaps you need to fill to become ready-now for your next role

- Who can help you verify your gaps?
- Which gaps are you most motivated to fill?
- What have you learned from your past which will help with filling one or more of your gaps?
- Which gap will you most appreciate some help with filling? Who can help?
- Which gaps are related to a personal strength being too-strong?

4 What you will begin to do and will stop doing

- On a scale of 1 to 10, how committed are you to begin and continue these things?
- How strong is the connection between your gaps and the things which you will begin to do or will stop doing? What can you learn from this?
- Who else needs to see, hear or know you are starting and stopping these things?
- How do you feel about stopping the things you need to stop?
- How do you feel about starting the things you need to start?
- What else do you need to start doing? What might you be assuming?
- What else do you need to stop doing? What might you be assuming?

5 Your list of stages to help organise the changes you need to make

- How many stages are needed to break down the changes you need to make into manageable pieces?
- What are the key desired outcomes within each stage?
- What influences the completion dates you have chosen?
- Who do you need to talk to about this?
- How will your relationships benefit as you ask for help?
- How will having a plan make you feel?
- Who else will benefit from your plan?

6 What you will do first

- What is the outcome you want to achieve with your first step?
- How does the outcome of the first step fit into achieving what you've described in your plan's first stage?
- Who could help you make your first step more successful and speedy?
- If you challenged yourself, how fast could you complete the first step?
- How do you feel about completing your first step?
- What does completing your first step encourage you to do to prepare for your second step?

7 Monitoring your progress

- Who must you update about your progress so they can influence others to notice you are closer to being ready-now?
- Who else has an influence on your next role and how will you update them on your progress?
- If your progress is faster than you expected, what learning will you take?
- What implications may there be?
- If your progress is slower than you expected, what learning will you take?
- How will you decide what to do differently?
- How will you make monitoring your progress simple and effective?
- Who else can help you understand what progress you've made?
- How will you celebrate and share your achievements along the way?

Appendix 6

Am I Coaching or a Mentoring Manager? Questionnaire

Use our short questionnaire to discover your current, default management style and learn how flexing your personal style will benefit you and those around you.

Download the questionnaire from our website. You will find it in the resources section of **www.ccmrconsulting.com/books**

Alongside the questionnaire you'll find templates from the book which you can print, use to record your thoughts and decisions, and share with others.

You'll also have the opportunity to receive our tip sheet newsletter from time to time. Enjoy!

Index

Neil V Raval is an exec coach to senior leaders internationally. He leads personal and organisational development programmes, has an MBA and is a registered NLP practitioner. He says graduating as a Chemical engineer gave him the appreciation of practical, real-world approaches to success which can be repeated. He is a co-founder of CCMR Consulting and lives in the northwest of England, UK with his family and dogs. In the corporate world, Neil has extensive experience of manufacturing, research & development, project and change management. His personal time is spent singing, supporting the Scout movement and walking the dogs. Connect with Neil at neil.raval@ccmrconsulting.com or linkedin.com/in/neil-raval-320a303

David M Smith is an international exec coach, an educator in personal and organisational development and a writer. He says that graduating as an electronics engineer taught him how to identify the root of problems, create practical solutions and share them so that others can benefit too. David has corporate experience in senior global-leadership roles within information services and research and development and over 15 years' experience as a coach. He has worked in Japan, USA and UK and lives in northwest England, UK with his family and dog. In his personal time, he enjoys supporting his local church, hiking in the Derbyshire hills, wrestling with new technology and practising yoga as an antidote. David is a registered NLP Practitioner, PRINCE2 Practitioner and co-founder of CCMR Consulting.

Connect with David at david.smith@ccmrconsulting.com or linkedin.com/in/smithdavidm